Religion, Aging and Health: A Global Perspective

Compiled by the
World Health Organization

Religion, Aging and Health: A Global Perspective

Compiled by the World Health Organization

William M. Clements
Editor

The Haworth Press
New York • London

Religion, Aging and Health: A Global Perspective has also been published as *Journal of Religion & Aging*, Volume 4, Numbers 3/4 1988.

The Haworth Press, Inc., 12 West 32 Street, New York, NY 10001
EUROSPAN/Haworth, 3 Henrietta Street, London WC2E 8LU England

LIBRARY OF CONGRESS
Library of Congress Cataloging-in-Publication Data

Religion, aging, and health : a global perspective / William M. Clements, editor.

    p. cm.
  Also published as Journal of religion & aging, volume 4, numbers 3/4 1988'' – T.p. verso.
    Includes bibliographical references.
    ISBN 0-86656-803-4
    1. Aging – Religious aspects. 2. Aged – Health and hygiene. I. Clements, William M.,
1945-   .
BL65.A46R44   1988
291.1'783426 – dc 19   88-16357
                                                   CIP

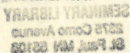

Religion, Aging and Health: A Global Perspective

CONTENTS

ABOUT THE EDITOR

William M. Clements, PhD, is Director of Behavioral Science, Family Practice Residency Program, at The Medical Center in Columbus, Georgia. He is also Associate Professor and Pastoral Counselor at the Emory University School of Medicine in Atlanta, Georgia. Dr. Clements, whose specialties are in religion, gerontology, and medicine, has published articles in leading religious and medical journals. He is a diplomate of the American Association of Pastoral Counselors and a minister in the United Methodist Church. Dr. Clements is the editor of the *Journal of Religion & Aging*.

Preface

Stimulated by the movement to attain health for all people by the year 2000, the World Health Organization launched a worldwide programme in the 1980s to promote and protect the health of elderly persons.

All countries of the developed world have health and social programmes for their senior citizens. These are long established and have often evolved from altruistic actions inspired by the predominating moral and religious beliefs of the society.

Services and programmes for elders in developing countries are likely to arise by a similar process, depending on the particular cultural, religious or social pattern.

In both developed and developing countries, national programmes for elderly people are directed towards maintaining wellbeing in the three dimensions defined in the WHO Constitution, namely physical, mental and social. In 1984, the Organization's Member States discussed extending this broad definition even further, to include a spiritual dimension. They argued that ennobling spiritual beliefs had given birth to the Organization's ideals of health equity and that these beliefs continue to motivate people to maintain wellbeing at different stages of the lifespan.

By the year 2000, some six hundred million elderly people will inhabit the earth, the great majority within developing societies that have dominant religious cultures—Hinduism, Buddhism, Islam, Christianity and others. Any erosion of the lifestyles and the traditional behaviour associated with these religions will have consequences for the wellbeing of the older members of the society.

Permission to publish this material has been granted by the World Health Organization.

The purpose of this publication is therefore to identify those elements of tradition, behaviour and lifestyle that are health protective in that, by adhering to them, physical, mental and social wellbeing will be maintained as people grow old, and culturally relevant health policies will be developed.

The World Health Organization identified contributors to this volume, with the assistance of the staff of its six regional offices. The Organization is grateful to the contributors who are identified with the relevant chapter heading. The solicited contributions were then edited by Dr. William Clements, Editor of the *Journal of Religion & Aging*, to whom the Organization is indebted for bringing the volume to publication.

The publication offers a global perspective to religion, aging and health which is of relevance to all generations, not only to elderly people.

David M. Macfadyen
Chief, Health of the Elderly
World Health Organization

Behavior, Lifestyle, Religion, and Aging in a Global Perspective: An Introduction

William M. Clements

Many factors influence human aging and longevity. Among these are phenomena such as culture, disease, nutrition, shelter, hygiene, genetics, religion, and education. The influence that each factor has on lifestyle, behavior and aging can be extraordinarily complex. These influential factors do not operate in isolation from all other matters that shape lifestyle, behavior and aging. At any one time in any single human life there is an enormously complex interrelationship between hundreds of variables. The task of describing these variables and isolating them from the context in which they naturally appear is a highly abstract activity. In order to accomplish the task of description scholars must choose some significant variables and ignore hundreds of others that undoubtedly have important influences on human behavior, lifestyle, and aging. (See Figure 1.)

In this monograph, authors have reflected on *religious* phenomena as they interact with behavior, lifestyle and human aging in several cultures. Each religion, however, is found within a distinct set of cultural circumstances. These circumstances modify, enhance, and ameliorate various tenets of any particular religion. For example, the Buddhism found in Thailand might differ remarkably from the Buddhism found in China. Or the Protestantism of a tribal village in Africa might differ significantly in its influence on behavior, lifestyle and aging from that Protestantism found in Northern

---

Permission to publish this material has been granted by the World Health Organization.

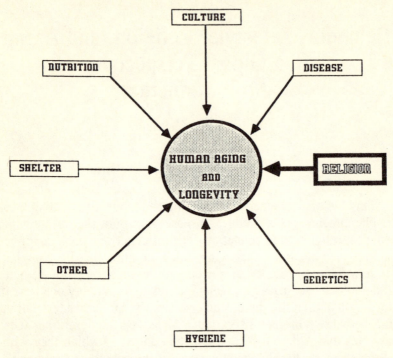

FIGURE 1. Some Variables Interacting with Human Aging and Longevity

Europe. So, religion itself is not a pure phenomenon that remains untouched by the culture within which it flourishes. The interrelationship between religion and culture, is however, a subject that is far beyond the scope of the present study to explicate and illuminate, yet this relationship is a reality that one must keep in mind when reading each of the following chapters. (See Figure 2A.)

There are innumerable ways for the reader to "get inside" a religious tradition and attempt to understand that religion. Our authors have each used a slightly different methodology in order to understand and explicate the religious phenomena about which they are writing. For example, one could take the practices found in any single religious tradition and describe the entire tradition in terms of these normative practices, such as liturgical practices (or worshiping practices), dietary practices, or beliefs about disease and illness. Or, one could take the core ideals of a particular religious tradition,

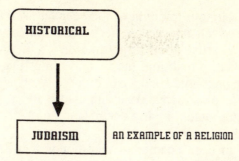

FIGURE 2A. A Particular Approach That Facilitates Religious Understanding

such as a tradition which values human life above other ideals, and examine this religious tradition on the basis of those ideals which motivate behavior and lifestyle decisions in a particular cultural context. On the other hand, one might choose to describe a tradition on the basis of that tradition's history, particularly as this history interacts with behavior, lifestyle and human aging.

Every religious tradition has a long and significant history that contains many notable events, paradigms and stories. Or, one could choose to describe and explicate the various stories and parables that are significant within a particular tradition, or one might compare a particular religious tradition with various other traditions, thereby shedding light on the indexed tradition by comparison with similar aspects from other traditions. Or, one could simply discuss human aging, behavior, and lifestyles from the personal experience and reflection of an individual who has lived within a particular cultural tradition. In other words, it could be a personal description from the standpoint or the viewpoint of one individual living within a particular setting in a particular time in history. Another illuminating approach would be to describe and set in the proper context the various sacred writings of a particular tradition that reflect on behavior and lifestyle as these phenomena interact with human aging. Another approach might begin with the personal meaning, the existential meaning, of a particular religious tradition and describe the way in which this religious tradition provides a sense of meaning, a sense of direction, to humans who live within it and apply its teachings to their own lives and their own society. Still another valid way of describing a religious tradition would be in terms of its ethics, the proper way in which one makes decisions, and the hierarchy of values within a particular religious tradition. Or, one could talk about the beliefs of a tradition, the various things that the tradition teaches that persons should believe in order to be an adherent of that tradition. Beliefs about deity, about humanity, and about the world are all significant factors in any understanding of human behavior and lifestyle. (See Figure 2.)

The authors of each chapter in this monograph have chosen a dominant methodology through which to approach a particular religious tradition. For example, the author of the chapter on the particular religious tradition Judaism, chose an historical method as an

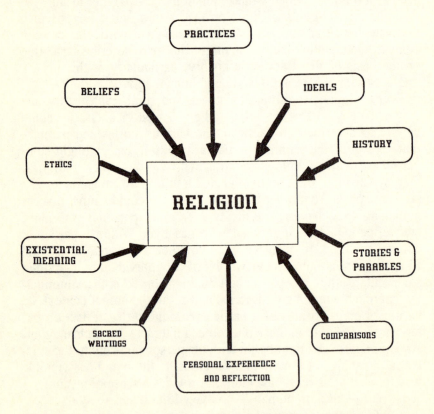

FIGURE 2. Some Approaches That Facilitate Religious Understanding

approach that would facilitate the readers' understanding of this tradition as it affects lifestyle, behavior, and human aging. Each particular religion can be understood from this historical perspective. (See Figure 3.)

An author can use an historical approach not just to describe the history of the tradition, but to describe how this religion interacts with human aging and longevity and behavior and lifestyle. Thus, historical methodology is one approach that facilitates understanding of a religious tradition in relationship to human aging and longevity. (See Figure 4.)

At this point, the reader is undoubtedly aware that many valid approaches to the same religion are entirely possible. For example, Judaism could be studied not only for an historical standpoint, but also from the standpoint of its sacred writings, or from a standpoint that describes the lifestyle associated with it. One should keep in

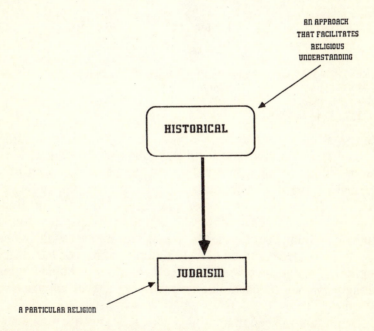

FIGURE 3. Each Religion Is Understood Through a Methodology or Approach Chosen by the Author

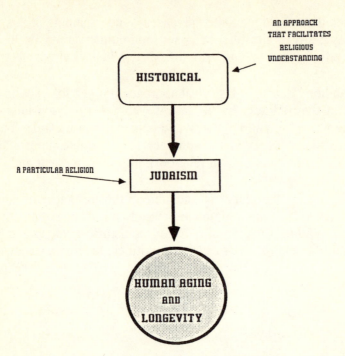

FIGURE 4. One Author's Approach to a Particular Religion as This Religion Interacts with Human Aging and Longevity

awareness at all times that many approaches to the same religious phenomenon are possible and valid and valuable. (See Figure 5.)

Another thing to keep in mind is that the same approach may be applied to a variety of religions. In other words, one might approach Buddhism from the standpoint of the lifestyle of Buddhists—to describe accurately the dominant lifestyles found throughout Buddhist cultures as these lifestyles interact with human aging; or, lifestyles could be used to describe Shinto or Islam, for example. Thus, the involvement of each religion in human aging and longevity may be examined through a variety of approaches. (See Figure 6.)

It is important to keep in mind that each religious tradition could be described from the standpoint of at least seven methodologies. In other words, Judaism could be discussed in terms of comparisons

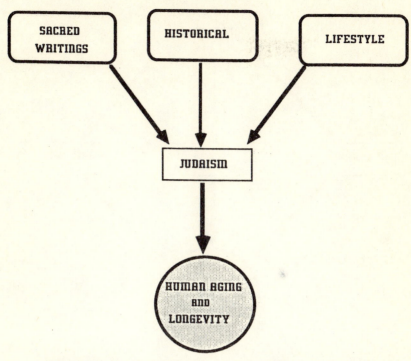

FIGURE 5. Many Approaches to the Same Religion Are Possible

with other religions or in terms of its history, its teleology, its stories and parables, its lifestyles, its ethical dimensions, its sacred
writings, or reflection on personal experience. In the wheel appear-
ing in Figure 7, if each methodology were simply rotated in a clock-
wise fashion, one could begin to appreciate the potential complexity
of the task at hand. Fortunately, each of our authors has chosen to
approach his or her religious tradition through one particular methodology. Generally speaking, they have each chosen different
methodologies to illuminate their particular traditions. Thus, the
reader can experience a variety of approaches without being inun-
dated by complexities. The cultural understanding of behavior, lifestyle, and aging is greatly facilitated by this volume. When one
considers it in its entirety, one can begin to grasp how various religious traditions have reflected upon the phenomena of human aging

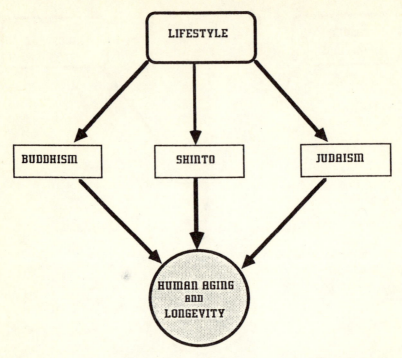

FIGURE 6. The Same Approach May Be Applied to a Variety of Religions

and how each of the various traditions has chosen to enhance the life experience of human aging. Each culture or religious tradition is limited in terms of its ability to grasp and explicate the entire phenomena. However, knowledge about and reflection on traditions other than one's own can greatly enrich and enhance those values and lifestyles and religious traditions that contribute to a meaningful advance into old age.

In "Lifestyles Leading to Physical, Mental and Social Wellbeing in Old Age," Paul Tournier writes from within the humanist tradition, using the methodology of personal experience and reflection. He lifts up for our consideration the importance of physical activity, and of mental activity, decrying the boring nature of a rigid routine and emphasizing a positive mood, curiosity, and social activity as themes which contribute to a positive process of aging.

Hakim Mohammed Said uses the sacred writings of Islam to dis-

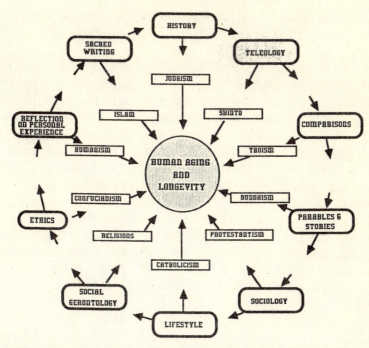

FIGURE 7. The Involvement of Each Religion in Human Aging and Longevity May Be Examined Through a Variety of Approaches

cuss various tenets that relate to the elderly and aging in Islamic society. Solidarity with the elderly and service to parents and respect for elders are concepts found in Islamic writings in which parents are co-equal to the old and infirm, who have various designated rights. When speaking about service to parents, one is also speaking about service to the old and the infirm whether or not the old and infirm person is one's biological parent. Mohammed Said presents the notion that the rite of throwing the elderly over the mountainside is still practiced in societies in which the elderly are separated from younger people through hospitalization or confinement to homes for the aging against, presumably, the elderly person's will.

Using stories and parables, Daw Khin Myo Chit teaches many of the essentials of Buddhism in regard to aging and the elderly, especially as they are expressed in Thailand. In a society in which seniority is important, matters of age do not tend to go unnoticed. Stories teach the young respect for elders and the traditions of a society in which respect is paramount.

In their discussion of Protestantism found in the rural South of the United States, Rebecca Adams and Bonnie Stark utilize the methodologies of sociology to study differences in services offered to the elderly. Within religious communities in a rural North Carolina county, conservatism is divided into doctrinal conservatism and social conservatism. Socially conservative churches are found to provide fewer services for the elderly in this population.

In his discussion of Judaism, Michael Davies uses a historical perspective to develop the term ''elder'' in the definition of aging, describing the characteristics of elderly people as seen in earlier historical times. Characteristic attitudes toward honor and support, religious burial, work and retirement, and the duties of the elder are discussed as they relate to the history of the development of various Israeli social institutions such as the Hakdesh Hospital and Old Age Home and the kibbutz.

In describing the teachings of Confucianism on health, Takehiko Okada shows that Confucian teaching about health follows from a moralistic view of life, of society and of the world in general. In Confucianism, to lead a good life and to help others lead a good life are closely related to each other because Self and Other are regarded as one. From the moralistic standpoint, benevolence is seen as the highest virtue, containing all other virtues. Almost as important is the virtue of gratitude — gratitude for one's elders, for a stable government, for health, and for the universe.

Carmen Barros points out that Catholicism has little to say about physical wellbeing directly. Instead, Catholicism has a great indirect effect through other factors such as the attitude of charity that reinforces social solidarity and through the definition of other people in family terms. Catholicism values all of life because it is a gift from God. The prime influence of Catholicism on human lifestyles is achieved through mental constructions and is exerted at the psychological level of human existence.

Professor Fukui elucidates a Taoist view of the health and wellbeing of the elderly by tracing the development of Taoist belief in the supremacy of the natural law (TAO) and the rise of the idea that human life could be extended forever by following the Tao.

Thus, longevity was pursued by means of thorough specific practices, leading to good health, including diet, exercise, and right relationships, and proper mental attitudes. In beginning his discussion of Shinto, Takeshi Mitsuhashi states that death presents a fundamental problem with regard to the elderly; to promote and preserve their health despite its closeness. Shinto, he says, offers a way of life which frees one from the fear of death and its loneliness. Shinto rites celebrate renewal and Shinto philosophy emphasizes the coexistence, or coequality, of all living things, as well as a life of simple sincerity.

Jeffrey Levin utilizes a social gerontological perspective to review six theoretical viewpoints that have guided empirical research into religion and health among aging people in the United States. He concludes that a multidimensional disengagement perspective comes closest to predicting the way in which religion and health are interrelated as persons age. While the populations studied have been predominantly Catholic or Protestant, identical theories might be applied to populations with other religions.

The cultures and religions of the world are many and various — and we all too often tend to focus on our differences. We need reminders of our similarities. In sponsoring this collection of thoughts from many cultures and religion, the World Health Organization has offered us an unusual opportunity to examine from many points of view to a single issue of worldwide concern, the health and well being of the elderly. The differences are obvious, and the similarities are startling — whether one's approach is historical, comparative, ethical, theological, or existential; whether one's viewpoint is Shinto, Taoist, Buddhist, Catholic, Islamic, Judaism, or humanist. Proper diet and adequate physical exercise are obviously vital to the health of the elderly. Equally vital are the psychological components of well being — a sense of usefulness, a feeling of kinship, of relationship, with others, a recognition of one's part in the continuity of life. Virtually every society faces, or will shortly face, the rapid growth of an elderly population, and its accompanying problems. We need to know that at best our basic values do not differ significantly in this area. The groundwork for cooperation lies ready within each culture, awaiting recognition.

Lifestyles Leading to Physical, Mental and Social Wellbeing in Old Age

Paul Tournier

The most important thing in the context of wellbeing in old age is that old people, despite their age, should remain as active as possible, physically, mentally and in their social life. They cannot be said to be given much incentive for that! There is a general tendency to associate the ideas of old age and of rest. Now, life is movement, evolution, metabolism, creation. Rest does exist in Nature, but always as a temporary state: night between two days, winter before the spring. Continuous rest rapidly leads to decline and precipitates decay.

The harmful effect of this idea of rest has been made worse in the industrial countries by the fairly recent institution of retirement. When a group reaches retirement age, a ceremony, with presentations and speeches, is held in the work place. Those who are retiring are thanked for their good and faithful service and wished "a well deserved rest." Although it is certainly deserved, it is highly dangerous if indulged in for too long. They would be better advised to look for some activity of use to society and within their capacity. To do something different from the work that leaves one tired out is a more effective way of recuperating than prolonged idleness.

Moreover, so saying is suggestive of a serious confusion between "retirement" and "old age," as if to retire were to signify being old! With the exception of a few very arduous professions that lead to premature aging, most workers are still in full possession of their physical, mental and social capacities on retirement. The proof of

Permission to publish this material has been granted by the World Health Organization.

this is that they all had responsible jobs only the day before. The abrupt transition from being fully active to a state of total inactivity is completely contrary to the laws of Nature which, as had already been said in Antiquity, "does not make leaps."

There are countless retired people fit for work who are struggling against boredom and who feel themselves suddenly to be on the scrap heap. This is a social problem; it is not only their misfortune, but also society's; a "waste," to use the expression of Professor Eric Martin.

Retirement is not old age. Why do we use the term "old-age pension" when we should be saying "retirement pension"? Old age will come gradually, slowly, perhaps 20 to 25 years later, or even longer, when a serious disability will make the individual unable to carry on normal activity. After these years in which all stimulation has been lacking, the individual will be physically and mentally far older. Many of the old people who have to be admitted to overcrowded convalescent homes would undoubtedly have been able to live several more years of independent life if their vitality had been sustained by absorbing occupations.

I am 87 years old, I have been receiving what is called an old-age pension for 24 years, and I still act as a consultant, give conferences, write books, and now this report for WHO. I have, undoubtedly, been lucky, but who would fail to see that this work helps to keep me young and that this youthfulness of spirit enables me to remain active? I am not the only one! Just think of Mao Tse-Tung, Adenauer, Casals, Goya, Verdi and many others who were still most productive when older than I.

This stupid problem of the idleness of the retired is one that primarily affects the industrialized West. The situation is quite different in Africa and the East. In China, the family, which is such a solid foundation of society, is not reduced to father, mother and the children (the number of whom is now limited). There are grandparents, uncles, aunts, great uncles and aunts, distant relatives and their offspring; there are so many of them that one has to use numbers: first uncle, second uncle, etc. Throughout this world, the oldest have all sorts of occupations that free the parents of "working" age. They have daily contact with the children and pass on to them their experience and their philosophy of life.

There is, however, an even more subtle and deep cause of this contrast between the continents: the whole of the West is dedicated to competition, which begins in school and impregnates the whole of working life, business and culture. Everything is competition: economic, political, sporting, artistic and scientific. When the individual is of working age, it is stimulating; the strong triumph and rush of the weak who become a charge on the State. Competition is life for the industrialized West! Retired persons are excluded from competition by virtue of being old; the last thing they should do is to compete with the working population. But what happens? No more competition, no more life! The old feel themselves to be rejected by the competitive society. One flogs oneself to death working for 45 years and thereafter dies of boredom.

The East has a quite different ideal — that of harmony, harmony between the Yin and Yang, which are mutually supportive and complementary. Harmony has something to do with the physical, mental, and social wellbeing propounded by WHO — physical, mental and social harmony and, in the final analysis, harmony between these three aspects of existence. This quest for harmony does not cease with retirement and old age. Quite the contrary! It was difficult to attain when overburdened during working life. Its importance becomes overriding for a happy old age. May not this harmony be a definition of lifestyles favorable to old age? WHO justifiably calls attention to the fact that health is not merely the absence of disease, but a feeling of wellbeing and harmony, since bodily health is not a static state, but a constantly readjusted balance between opposing and complementary functions such as the effects of the sympathetic and parasympathetic nervous systems.

This brings me back to my starting point, which was to remain active insofar as possible. What is needed is harmony between activity and rest, neither too much nor too little, in accordance with age and with physical, mental, and social capacities. We need to get away from the conflict between people of working age who are overloaded and people who are retired and deprived of work!

PHYSICAL ACTIVITY

Let us start with physical activity: it is of prime importance in advancing age. This has been seen with the establishment of courses in gymnastics for the elderly, new leases on life for old people who had resigned themselves to staying in their armchairs. It is, of course, not competitive gymnastics, but gymnastics harmoniously adapted to the needs of each individual. There is also the swimming pool, which has the great merit of bringing the old into contact with the young.

Next, let us take walking. It is the natural form of physical exercise, ideal at any age and easy not to overdo. The young of today have no idea of how much we walked at the beginning of the century. The advent of the private car has had regrettable consequences for health. A car can be justified when one is working, but there are some retired people who use the car to go out for a newspaper when they really do have the time to walk. Harmony means doing away with this obsession with saving time. It is a curious fact that as people have invented machines to save time — the car, the airplane, the typewriter, the calculator, the photocopier, all the way to the computer — they have become increasingly in a hurry. It must be something in them. Our patients obey us more readily when we prescribe medicine than when we ask them to walk for an hour a day.

To make an example, I have a patient with rheumatism. He walks less and less because it hurts; but the less he walks, the more his joints seize up. Such vicious circles are to be found in all areas of medicine. Courage is needed to break away from them insofar as possible, but to do so is of the greatest importance in struggling against aging. As is clearly shown by paleontology, any organ that ceases to function atrophies. An industrialist once said to me: "Retirement is no problem, all you have to do is to get up at the same time as when you went to the office." That is, of course, an exaggeration but it has a kernel of truth. Harmony calls for constant adjustment of the daily timetable. Although there may be less to do, it should not be too much less.

Old people have less money, but more time, and the saying "Time is money" also relates to them. An elderly lady may not be able to buy as many dresses, but with a little perseverance she does have the time to alter old ones. She is then visibly radiant because she has succeeded in doing something that she had never done before; she has developed. Life is always in evolution.

An old man has the time to wander round the market and to buy healthier foods than the tinned foods that he used to buy in the supermarket, and to pay less. His finds are a source of pleasure to him. All these household activities maintain physical condition. I have been a widower for ten years, and the fact of doing my own shopping and cooking has been of help to me in my loneliness. There is also the time to vary menus, to try out or invent new recipes, or to go on a diet, and any ingenuity contributes to the harmony of existence. Except during adolescence, most people overeat. This is especially so of the elderly, when meals become their main distraction.

I should also like to mention care of the person. My colleague, Professor Hugonot, of Grenoble, told me that when he opened a beauty salon for the elderly, it was amazingly successful. With her hair well done, with a manicure and perfume, an elderly lady comes out rejuvenated in body and mind, full of confidence in herself. Old people often complain of not being respected. In order to be so, we must respect ourselves, and how we look is an expression of that. Once again, this has a bearing on the concern for harmony.

MENTAL ACTIVITY

The second point is mental activity. It is as important as physical activity in combating premature aging, and it is the complement to physical activity for personal harmony. In order to make a success of a career, every worker has to specialize increasingly and to narrow down the scope of thought. Many things in which the individual was interested when young have to be left in abeyance. In a society as compartmentalized and functional as ours, working life makes the individual something of a robot. Personal imagination really has little role to play in Western industrialized society. In their book *The Lean Kine (Les vaches maigres)*, written after the economic crisis of 1973, Michel Albert and Jean Fernet maintain that we are wrong to regard our epoch as especially creative just because it is rich in invention: creativity is, in reality, the province of the few, the scientists of research departments and leading employers. What a difference there is between that and the time of the handicraft economy when everyone was required to use their brains. Now most workers have nothing but routine. Professor Arthur Jores, of Hamburg, who studied deaths following retirement, concluded that routine was the enemy. He said that the person in danger of dying was the one who had no other interest in life apart from work. The death rate is highest among workers whose occupations are the most routinely organized. Even if they do not die from their routine outlook, they will find it far more difficult to recover any youthfulness of spirit.

In a seminar on preparation for retirement, I spoke of the importance of reading to stimulate our mental activity. A senior bank employee then said, "I don't think that I've read a book in 20 years." He used to read the Stock Exchange prices and skim through a few papers. If you ask such a man to read a book, he will read a few pages and then he'll look at the end to see how many there are and will give it up discouraged. All beginnings are difficult for lack of practice, whether it be learning a foreign language, painting, gardening, the piano, goldsmithing, modern physics, computer science or heraldry. Furthermore, whatever a retired person undertakes, there will be friends to say, "There's no point in giving yourself so much trouble." This is because people are accustomed to regard study as a means to a career. It was to get on in the occupational hierarchy that one used to take evening courses. What point is there in old age? The answer is that it helps to rejuvenate, to develop oneself, to broaden one's interests, and to impart more harmony to life.

Furthermore, study can be carried out at leisure, peacefully, at one's own personal pace, with time ahead; think of what can be done in 20 years with serious application and not merely as a distraction. There is social esteem to be gained, which plays an important role in physical and mental health. Most retired people do not realize how privileged they are. They make a journey about which they have always dreamed, but on their return they still have as many years in front of them as the years of their youth when they were preparing for their working career. They then run the risk of squandering their energies on all kinds of futile things and of tiring rapidly instead of acquiring a skill that will open up a second career for them. For it is only ever at the cost of some effort that true satisfaction is found.

It cannot be too strongly recommended that everyone should take up a new activity even before retiring. This is why a chemical industry in my country already invites its staff to attend a stock-taking seminar at the age of 50. It was its director who, when he heard me stressing this early beginning of a new activity, at once had the idea of re-enrolling in the university to take a doctorate in economics and social science. Two years later, on retiring, he was able to devote himself to it full-time and get his doctorate. I saw him again recently, and he is being asked to hold conferences in industry, and has a completely new career. I myself was 42 when I published my first book without realizing that that was going to involve me in a whole career of authorship. It is mental activity that opens the way to practical action and practical action that maintains mental life and provides true prevention against premature decline.

One of my friends, a colonel who was keenly interested in matters military, could have been unhappy on retirement, but devoted his time to writing a history of the troops of his Canton. An old village priest, in retirement, produced a monograph on the history of the village whose priest he had been for so long. A tobacco factory, which organizes excellent seminars in preparation for retirement, arranges "botanical rambles" for its staff. Anyone who has been on a few of these rambles will find considerable interest in any future walk. A little science is needed to learn more, and life once again becomes an enthralling adventure. And it is never too late, as the prodigious success of the universities for the retired shows. The directors of large enterprises are always so absorbed in their immediate problems that they complain of having no time for long-term perspectives. Former directors who, although retired, are completely capable, can consider such perspectives at their leisure, without competing with anyone.

What matters in all this is mood, the disposition of the retired and of the old. Now mood counts a great deal for health. All sorts of indispositions, and even diseases, will soon establish themselves in a life devoid of stimulating interests, just as weeds spring up on land on which nothing is being grown. Of course, as in the case of physical activity, there is a proper, harmonious proportion for mental activity. It is no longer a hectic and competitive occupation, as it was during working life. But the person who stops using his brain, who no longer turns over projects in his mind, who ceases to consider theoretical or practical problems that need to be solved, loses his creative imagination, becomes passive and deteriorates at an increasing rate. Should illness then follow, there will be no resistance to it.

This phenomenon has to be understood: all the laws of Nature are cyclic. Eggs are needed to get chickens, and chickens to get eggs. Retirement is a kind of unhappy love affair. It is impossible to devote 40 years of one's life to an enterprise without becoming attached to it, even when one remains critical, even when one is tired and looks forward to retirement. All at once the enterprise discards you like an unfaithful lover, and gets on very well without you! More than that, you get told that some young person has replaced you, who understands electronics and who is dynamic to boot. Later on, as the aging process continues, it really will be necessary to say good-bye to many things to which one was attached. Unhappy love affair, bitterness, inevitable sorrow that it is good to be able to express, but beware of the vicious circle of bitterness. If you sit back in an armchair with a dissatisfied look and if, because of your bad temper, you say "what good will that do?" to every suggestion made to you, you will have nothing to say to a friend who comes to see you, apart from complaining, and it will probably be a long time before he comes to see you again. The less he comes, the more bitter you will become, and the more bitter you are, the less he will come.

A grandfather complained about his grandson, who very rarely came to see him. I spoke to the grandson, who answered me in a forthright manner:

> You know Doctor, it's no pleasure to go and see Grandfather. No sooner am I there than he gives me hell for having been so long in coming, and he criticizes my hairstyle, my clothes, everything; I tell myself that I would have done better not to have gone.

I was asked to speak about old age in a large college. I, who believed that young people disdained the old, realized that the opposite was the case. How they welcomed me! Many of these young people said how much they wished to establish contact with old people, to listen to them and understand them, and to assist them in small ways, for example by helping an old lady to cross the street at a crossroads, but the young girl who made that offer had been very badly received: "Nasty brat, look after your own affairs! I didn't ask you to do anything! Go away!" They all asked me why old people were so critical and sometimes detestable. I replied: "Probably through jealousy; not only because you have your life before you, while theirs is behind them, but also because you have a freedom that they lacked in their youth."

It is here that we come for a moment to the social activity to which I must refer later, but we need to see quite clearly that these misunderstandings and vicious circles have their roots in the mental activity and mood of the old. If they do not accept that they are old, if they are full of complaints and criticism, they become ever more embittered, passive, and on the decline. This difficulty in accepting the unacceptable is to be found in all areas of medicine. To begin with, no one really accepts illness or infirmity. There are those who pretend to do so, and so much the better for them, since they are coping. But on second thought, one has a choice: either to overcome one's indignation, or to let oneself go. In general, it is striking to see how much better young people cope. Everyone has seen young people who are condemned to spend the whole of their lives in wheelchairs but who are radiant, perhaps because of the daily effort to overcome their handicap. Old age is not an infirmity in itself, but it brings infirmities, and it is the inexorable decline that constitutes the handicap. Sacrifices do, in fact, have to be made throughout life, but in old age there are fewer external compensations, merely the possibility of internal development.

I think, for example, of two well-known footballers who have reached the age at which they are no longer picked for the big matches. One of them is so frustrated that he no longer even goes to matches. "It makes me too fed up," he says, "to see the others play when I can no longer play myself." And he may add, to justify his reaction: "Anyway, football isn't what it was: in my time we had ideals; now they only play for money." The other player goes to all the games; he congratulates his young comrades and gives them good advice, he remains popular, and will soon be made chairman of the club, which will be a whole new career.

What matters is our reaction to events, our state of mind, far more than the events themselves. Apart from desire, which has been so much investigated by psychologists, another of the main-springs of mental life is curiosity. There is, moreover, a link between the two. Think about the natural curiosity of the child. There is an age at which the child wears out the parents with questions. He or she is discovering life in all its absorbing richness, is bubbling over with life, and wants to become an astronaut, a famous painter, an inventor and a clown, all at the same time. What a contrast with the old person, whom the child will perhaps one day become, who is no longer interested in anything because of depression, and is depressed because of the loss of interest in anything. The reason is because society will have gradually taken away that person's curiosity. It began in school, when he was dreaming about what he was making with his Meccano set, and the teacher pulled him up sharply. He had to learn how to spell in order to be successful in life. Successful in his career, his working life, perhaps, but what about his old age? Society does not prepare us for old age because it exploits us for productive purposes.

SOCIAL ACTIVITY

And now to the last point: social activity. It, as we have seen throughout these pages, is dependent on physical and mental condition, but it also affects physical behavior and mental stimulation. A person who, for example, becomes a member of a choir engages in regular breathing exercises, which are very good for bodily health, develops musical appreciation, and establishes, week by week, links with a living community inspired by pursuit of a shared aim. The older the person becomes, the greater is the possibility of seeking this harmony between personal life and social life. At the height of the active period of life, there is a danger of being carried away by a mass movement, of losing all personal judgment. This has clearly been seen with Nazism. But there is also a risk, in the prevailing climate of competition in the West, of becoming an isolated individualist, alone against the world, cut off, devoid of a sense of community.

Such a person would do well to join the choir at the age of 40 or 50, rather than waiting until retirement. Then, by retirement, he or she will have generated sufficient enthusiasm not to miss rehearsals on some trifling pretext, and will be well integrated into the community and feel sufficient ties with friends within it to tolerate those who criticize. He or she will already have become a respected veteran. In addition, there are concerts abroad, trips that would not have been undertaken alone. There are, in addition, the applause of the public, the welcomeness of success and so on, which are also good for health.

Man is a social being and needs social esteem. If it be true that, as we have noted, retirement is an unhappy love affair, it also brings with it loss of social esteem, of "panache," as one of my friends told me at the height of depression from retirement. This is especially the case in the industrialized West, which is geared to production. The prestige of the enterprise is reflected on all who work in it, as they realize when they leave. In other continents, or in a craft economy, to the extent that it still exists and will perhaps be revived, the old are more respected. They are also less numerous, which is not a matter of indifference. Consider, for example, political refugees; when a few arrive, they are welcomed with open arms, but when they crowd in, they are very poorly received.

Then there is the question of money. The standing of people in all countries is more or less connected with what they spend. It is prestige that makes people in modest circumstances give expensive presents to their children. The amount of pocket money that young people have today would have seemed magical when I was a child. It has made them the subject of attention; they are taken seriously by commercial specialists, and they represent a sizeable market, especially because they are more capable of being influenced by advertising. The improvements that have been made in old age pensions do not merely save retired persons from poverty, but also improve their social standing, which is very good for morale and, consequently, for health. But we have a long way to go. I know of only one enterprise whose retired employees receive as much in pension as their final paypacket, provided that they have worked there for 30 years. They should in fact have even more, since we all know that we spend more when on holiday. Retired people are recommended to ski and to play tennis and golf to keep in condition, but to do so costs money.

Luckily, there are social activities that cost nothing, more particularly ordinary conversation and personal encounter. The individual has to have the right disposition, however. This brings us up against the very character of the elderly person. One of the main problems of old age, as everyone knows, is loneliness. Why did not many of those who complain of loneliness form contacts with other lonely people when they were still able to, even on a park bench? There are some people who strike up a conversation immediately, and others who do not. This is an important difference. But it is not enough to open up: the decisive factor is mood, state of mind, as I have said. If each of the people concerned talks only about his or her own woes, the meeting is scarcely likely to result in a lasting friendship, as could be the case were each to be interested in the other. The driving force of this interest is love of people and of things. The whole of my career has taught me that our technical and functional civilization is very little conducive to deep contact. Many many patients have told me of working for years in a workshop or office without any superior or colleague ever taking an interest in their personal life, but only in their output.

I hope that there will not be any misunderstanding. I am a doctor and I am well aware there are circumstances that lead to solitude without the victim being in any way responsible: these include widowhood, the death of old friends, family quarrels and weaknesses. Nevertheless, there are many old people who have, without realizing the fact, been parties to if not directly responsible for, the progressive isolation from which they suffer. They received letters that they failed to answer, they did not pay visits when they were able to do so, and they tend to withdraw into their shells and are unsociable by nature or under the influence of a cold society that they themselves should have helped to make warmer. They previously opted for solitary amusements and hobbies when there are collective ones that establish lasting links. One finds, for example, members of the Club Alpin who faithfully attend its meetings, despite the fact that their age makes it no longer possible for them to take any trip in the mountains.

I spoke just now of a choir; there are many other societies, clubs, and political, trade union, religious, and cultural movements. The lonely were too individualistic to involve themselves when they were younger. That is why I spoke at the outset of remaining active at all ages insofar as possible. Being active is not just doing something, but becoming involved. It is through this involvement that one makes new friends. It is this commitment that gives a meaning to life, because it is no longer only a matter of entertainment. In the final analysis, it is even possible to remain active without doing anything, as some cheerful invalids do. All that matters in old age is to stop giving the orders. The mother-in-law who thinks that she can tell her daughter-in-law how to run her house will become estranged, as will a former manager who presses his advice on his successor.

It is also so that they should remain active that, in general, old people are left independent in their homes for as long as possible. The fact of entering an old people's home, apart from having a disorienting effect, very often causes an old person to relapse dangerously into a passive state through the loss of feeling of personal responsibility and of being able to some extent to provide for his or her needs. This might perhaps be altered, since great progress has been made in the attitude towards old people's homes in recent years. They were formerly large, barrack-like places in which a half of the pensioners died during their first year, as had been revealed by Simone de Beauvoir. They were situated outside town so that the pensioners could have the benefit of the fresh air, but in places where it was difficult for their friends and relations to visit them, and where there was no entertainment.

Nowadays the policy is to increase the number of small homes more conducive to a feeling of personal privacy and a lively, communal existence, despite the inevitable jealousies between old people who no longer have much to increase their standing. But above all there is an attempt to liven up these old people's homes, to organize games, concerts, talks, and discussions. I have met young people who were devoting themselves entirely to this noble effort, but it could, with a little training, be a marvelous occupation for people who, although old, are not too old and are still capable. In that case pensioners might find a social climate that was more stimulating than life on their own, and where they would have a healthier diet and some cultural and spiritual development.

CONCLUSION

Life is always evolution, growth and movement, movement of the mind if bodily movement is hampered. I have been at pains to demonstrate that the laws of Nature are such that each stage helps to determine the following stages, that there is a unity to life, that old age is the fruit of the whole of existence, and that the individual is preparing for it at all ages through his or her behavior, through the way in which he or she reacts to successive events, and through the view of the world and of life arrived at through personal thought and encounters with inspired people.

Islam and the Health
of the Elderly

Hakim Mohammed Said

SUMMARY. When there is any talk of action for the health care of the aged in the light of the teachings of Islam, we will naturally have to keep in view basically all those aspects of Islamic society which are related to the family system, self respect, and economy. Not only this, but we will also have to take into account all those Islamic concepts which are related to human dignity and which explicitly demand that man should be considered as a man and should be loved. We will adopt the same line of thought in this article.

It is Allah Who
Created you in a State
Of (helpless) weakness, then
Gave (you) strength after weakness,
Then, after strength, gave (you)
Weakness

al-Quran: Rum, XXX:54

The various stages of biological changes in man to which this *Ayat* refers reflect God's omnipotence in the sense that it is He who pulls man out of childhood weakness and frailty and gives him the strength and power of youth and then leads him to old age. And the One who has command over this creation and transformation has also the divine power to lead men to life after death. The *Ayat* also points to the fact that irrespective of any division of men into classes and groups in terms of age or strength, weakness or power,

---

Permission to publish this material has been granted by the World Health Organization.

the Creator of all is, in fact, one God and it is He who divides men into classes by leading them to the different stages of strength. Thus, the basis of creation is common and the caravans of the young and the old are heading towards the same goal. Hence this change of condition cannot separate them and make them indifferent to each other. They are in fact members of the same human race, and since all are the creation of the same Creator, they cannot be differentiated on the basis of change in apparent condition. In an Islamic society an old person has as much right to safety of life and property as a young man has. All those basic rights that Quran gives to man are available to a person in every stage of life. In fact, they have greater significance in old age.

A unique distinction of an Islamic society is that it has given full security to a man who makes his journey from the cradle to the grave, whether he is a child or a youth or an old and disabled person. For this security, the Holy Quran has given the concept of inviolability of life and has said:

> If anyone slew
> A person — unless it be
> For murder or for spreading
> Mischief in the land —
> It would be as if
> He slew the whole people:
> And if anyone saved a life,
> It would be as if he saved
> The life of the whole people.

Another concept is that of family and collective life under which the need for better treatment of relatives has been emphasized and the parents have been given paramount importance. If Islam did not want to promote family life, it would not have underscored the need for better treatment of parents and relatives. Hence, in my view, this concept of domestic life has basic importance so far as economic, material, and physical security of the different classes of men is concerned.

The third concept relates to surety and responsibility. In an Islamic society, an individual is not only responsible for his own needs but he has been told, "And there is a fixed share of the poor and the deprived in their wealth." At another place, it has been said, "And give the relative his right."

From these and other similar *Ayats*, it is clearly evident that Islam is a supporter of family life and is a standard bearer of self respect. Its economic system is based on collective responsibility. On these bases, it provides security to all classes and determines the rights and duties of each group separately.

There is no exaggeration in the fact that it is the Quran which has most vividly laid stress on the rights of the old and disabled in human society. It must be made clear here that in this context the Quran has used constitutional, or legal, language. It is perhaps more appropriate to say that it has used symbolic style for emphasizing the rights of parents. It is a noteworthy feature of Quranic sequence that immediately after laying stress on submission to Him and Him alone, God Almighty said without any introduction:

> Thy Lord hath decreed
> That ye worship none but Him,
> And that ye be kind to parents
> Whether one or both of them attain
> Old age in thy life.
> Say not to them a word
> Of contempt, nor repel them,
> But address them
> In terms of honor.
> And, out of kindness,
> Lower to them the wing
> Of humility, and say:
> "My Lord! bestow on them
> Thy mercy even as they
> Cherished me in childhood."

Bani Israil XVII:23,24

The purpose of this *Ayat* is to drive home that fact that while generally all human beings have an obligation to each other, the parent's right is paramount. Hence the collective ethic of the society should be such that it should not make children indifferent to parents; rather, they should be obedient, obliging, ready-to-serve, and duty-conscious. They should consider service to parents in old age as necessary since they were supported in childhood.

In the above lines it has been said that service to parents, good treatment to them, being kind and mild to them, etc., have been described in a constitutional language.

In fact, within the extended family in which a man lives, the parents enjoy the most important position with respect to age and status. "Old age" has been explicitly mentioned in the above *Ayat*, one of the main reasons for the injunction being to treat parents with respect in their old age, their weakness and disability. If the *Ayat* were studied carefully, its various sentences would reveal that in fact their old age and disability is the most valid reason for showing them respect and kindness. For example, "Say not to them a word of contempt, be kind to them." Just think that at what stage of life people become so infirm and doting that both children and youths feel displeased to meet or serve them and consider them insane and senile. They even scold them. This stage of life is called old age, the age of infirmity and disability. Hence the conclusion can be drawn that whosoever is so infirm and weak, whether he is a parent or not, should get this same treatment of love and respect, for Islam does not only consider the old and disabled a member of society but treats him as a respectable citizen. Islam has ordered that he be given due respect not only on moral grounds but also has provided legal security to him through the law of inheritance. He may not be able to move his lips but he cannot be deprived of his property in his lifetime. By fixing various people's shares in his property Islam has also legally made them an instrument of service to the old so that they may prove themselves his rightful heirs. Morally there can be no greater ungratefulness than that a man should neglect and despise an old person whose heir he is. That is why Islam has protected the rights of the old both morally and legally. On the basis of this law, a material cause has been created to serve the old. The foundation of responsibility, inviolability of life, and family system that Islam has laid constitutionally for these rights is very significant and meaningful. It will not be out of place to make brief references to their meaningfulness.

From the Islamic point of view, responsibility means that every individual of Islamic society and all the men in authority are collectively responsible to see that nobody, regardless of caste or creed, should remain unfed, unclad, and uncared for in sickness. Besides, if anybody died in a state of helplessness because of old age and disability, then all the members of the society would be implicated and held responsible for his death before God. I would like to explain this point here through an example:

> Imam Abu Yusuf has written in his book *Kitab al-Kharaj* that a group of seven persons on a journey reached a village. Not only were they extremely thirsty but their cattle were also dying of thirst. There was a pond in front of them. When they made their way towards it to quench their thirst, as well as that of their cattle, the village people interrupted them, surrounded the pond, and started shooting arrows. The thirsty souls withdrew disappointedly and encamped in the field. Some of the cattle survived, but most of the travelers succumbed to the intensity of thirst during the night. When the news-writer informed the Caliph Omar, he declared the whole settlement as murderers and said that the entire population would have to pay *Diya* (blood money).

It can be very well understood from this example that it is incumbent on every Muslim, rather every citizen of an Islamic state, to provide the means of livelihood to another citizen. Provision of medicine is an absolute imperative. Similarly, to help the old and disabled is binding and is a religious duty. When one person fulfills it, it means that the entire Islamic society has done its duty.

In the beginning of this article it was said that the word *parents* has been used symbolically for old and infirm people. There is no denying that after God and the Holy Prophet, it is parents who have the greatest right. But the fact is that in an Islamic society, every old and disabled person deserves the same respect, compassion, and solicitude that the parents do because Islam stands guarantor to the security of life and personal bail. And this guarantee is for every member of an Islamic society, whether Muslim or non-Muslim. I would like to quote another example from *Kitab al-Kharaj*.

Hazrat Omar passed by a blind Jew who was stretching his hand before people for alms. He reprimanded him and asked what had forced him to beg alms. When it was proved that he was reduced to begging because of old age, payment of *Jizya*, and blindness, Farooq-e-Asam said with great sorrow, "We must admit in clear words that we have not done justice to you. We received *Jizya* from you when you were young and strong, now when you have become old, we have left you completely helpless. By God, this is not justice, by God, this is not justice."

Saying this, he headed towards the *Bait al Mal* and ordered the name of the Jew to be noted and so much stipend to be given to him that the needs of his life may be met and he may not be compelled to beg.

After narrating this story, I need not explain that while the old and disabled persons socially deserve good treatment from family members and close relatives, which has also been described as an act of goodness by Islam, it is the job of government authorities to fix stipend for them from the *Bait al Mal* in case they cannot earn their livelihood because of old age and their children and relations are unmindful of their duty towards them. This is the right of every person who is a member of Islamic society, whether Muslim or non-Muslim. The present age has now realized the need for giving pensions to the old and making the government responsible for their sustenance.

The fact is that no government, even by giving pensions can give those rights and concessions to the old which Islam has given on moral and religious grounds because the problem of the old is not economic alone. Nor is it a problem of health or paucity of funds for their care. What is essential is an attitude of kindness and compassion towards them so that they may feel strong psychologically. Besides, it is necessary to be respectful, affable and polite to them and to obey their orders so that they may realize their importance in the family. They should not need to look for hired men to talk to as is happening in the West. Their relatives should collect around them, considering it an honor to listen to them.

A true idea of the rights that Islam has given to the old and disabled, the atmosphere of respect and compassion that it has created for them in society and the emphasis with which it has underscored the need for the security of their lives and for their personal prestige, can be had from a study of human history. It need not be stressed that man has passed through such a dark age that when old and disabled parents were considered a burden on society, they used to be thrown over the mountains so that the beasts might gobble them up or they might die their own deaths. You should not be surprised to know that this bloodcurdling atrocity used to be perpetrated not by others but by their own children. While in today's civilized world, though the savage custom of throwing over the mountains has been abandoned, the system of relegating the old to their fate by dumping them in hospitals or just forgetting them after consigning them to the homes for the aged does exist. Since the family system has been torn to pieces, even this job is performed either by the residents of the city or by the police. An old man has neither right of inheritance nor has he any status from the religious point of view. There is no moral compulsion on others either, for materially his existence and non-existence have become synonymous. In a materialistic society the concepts of human value or inviolability of soul are also materialistic. Evidently when an old person becomes physically infirm, sick, and dependent, he becomes worthless. This fact has been described by the Quran in these words: "Whomsoever I make old, I invert this constitution" (Yasin, XXXVI:68).

When an old person has lost his material value after becoming a victim of infirmity and weakness, why should the world pay attention to him? From an historical perspective, we should refresh the meaning of the Quranic *Ayats* in our minds. Islam told us for the first time that the importance of parents was only next to the unity of God and taught us to be good, polite, affable, and subservient to them. Thus, it not only established the image of the old but gave them due status and prestige in society. It described their existence as a source of blessing. God Almighty declared that their pleasure was His pleasure and their displeasure His wrath.

Hazrat Alquama's wife appeared before the Holy Prophet in a state of distress and said, "O God's Apostle! Alquama is sick. He is dying. But the trouble is that neither he can utter *Kalima* from his lips nor does he pass away." The Holy Prophet (peace be upon him) asked whether he had his mother. She replied in the affirmative. The Holy Prophet asked, "Does she remain angry with him?" She again replied in affirmative. The messenger of God himself asked the old mother to pardon Alquama. The moment she pardoned him, he died in peace, uttering *Kalima*. Islam has taught us that the parents' displeasure is man's greatest misfortune. Alquama's old mother had no material value, but by stressing her sanctity and sacredness this *Hadith* has proved that one's prestige does not depend on his or her physical strength but on the service that one has rendered.

According to a story in *Tafseer-e-Ibn-e-Kaseer*, as Hazrat Saad bin Abi Waqqas embraced Islam, his mother, who was a non-Muslim, gave up eating and drinking and said that unless he renounced Islam, she would not eat. Hazrat Saad said, "I don't care," and had harsh words for her. It is said in the Quran,

> It is correct that the words of polytheists and infidels will not be accepted, but it is the duty of the progeny to treat them (parents) well, which means that it should be polite and affable in talk to them.

According to another authentic tradition, a Muslim lady from Madinah said, "O messenger of God, my mother is an infidel and a destitute. She has come from Mecca. Can I help her?" The Holy Prophet replied, "Of course."

This throws into bold relief the peculiar temperament of Islamic society in which parents or old persons have been given a place of honor and security not only on one basis but on three grounds — religious, moral, and legal. Has the world presented such an example of such good treatment of the old and infirm in any period of history? And has their existence been considered so revered and respected?

Keep this *Hadith* also in view according to which God says that "Whoever respected an old Muslim, he respected Me!" It seems as if an old person reflects the glory of God. Insulting old men or showing indifference to them is a sign of arrogance which is not liked by God because it behooves only Him to be proud.

My writing will remain incomplete if I do not present the sayings of the greatest benefactor of mankind; the Holy Prophet (peace be upon him), about the old and disabled. An elaboration of these is essential in order to understand their place in an Islamic society.

According to *Abu Dawood*, Hazrat Abu Darda says, "I heard the Holy Prophet say that I like the old and infirm most because it is due to them that you get victory, and you get your maintenance also because of the old and weak persons!"

Another *Hadith* says "Treat the old well and be kind to the young." Good treatment includes politeness, affability and all other things which have been stressed by the Quran in the context of parents.

The Quran not only issued injunctions for treating the old well, but it also gave them liberal concessions in fulfilling religious duties, which proves that this is a class of men which, because of its old age and disability, not only merits special kindness and compassion but also deserves definite exemptions and concessions. For example, according to the Quran, if a person is too old and weak, he can give compensatory charity instead of fasting himself. If Haj is binding on him and he is old and disabled, he can send somebody else in his place for pilgrimage. He is exempted from attending the congregation. If he attends congregational prayers, then the Imam has been directed to be considerate to him.

The Holy Prophet said that anybody leading the prayer should make it short because the congregation includes the old, infirm and the sick. Albeit, when he prays alone, he can prolong the prayer as much as he wants. The exemptions that have been given to the old and disabled in respect of prayers and other religious duties prove that the old people are not considered a liability in an Islamic society. Instead of ridiculing them for their disability or showing indifference to them, Islam pays them special attention. All the injunctions and orders for the care and respect of the old and disabled are enough to understand that they have special rights in an Islamic society and old age need not be despised. In fact, according to the Quran, lesson should be taken from old age and it should be served.

When different sections of the *Bail al mal* (treasury) were established during the period of Second Caliph, Omar the Great, it included a department of pensions also. According to a story of *Kitab-ul-Amwal*, these pensions used to be given to the unemployed, old, and disabled persons as well as to other people. According to

Saad Hazrat, Omar bin Abdul Aziz took so much pains that he got a list of disabled persons in the entire country prepared and started paying stipend to them. His greater achievement, which symbolizes Islam's sense of responsibility in respect of the old and disabled and its compassion and solicitude for this particular section of the population, is that he built public kitchens at various places, together with serais and guest houses. He also wanted to raise buildings at different places for the people's regular stay, providing all the basic necessities, but the project did not see the light of the day because he did not last long. But the public kitchens have been mentioned by all the historians, including Ibn-e-Aseer and Ibne Kaseer.

The bases on which the Islamic culture is founded encompass all areas of life and cover the members of all classes. Take medical care as an example. By establishing a separate chapter on the hygienic rules for the old and disabled, the researchers of Islamic medicine have given proof of their professional expertise. In these chapters we get such directives about their care, food, etc. that we are compelled to believe that these experts of Tibb (medicine) had faith in the family system and considered the old and disabled honorable and illustrious members of the society. Their instructions about old people's health and hygiene are a testimony to the physician's belief that they are a blessing for the family. Such care should be taken of their health that they are saved from fatal diseases and have a long life according to God's will.

Not only in medicine but in many areas of art and letters, Avicenna can be called a spokesman of Islamic medicine and its social and cultural values. In his universally famous book "Canon of Medicine," he has talked about the old and disabled in detail in the context of hygiene. I present below some extracts from his chapters on food, bath, exercise, etc. Basically, it must be kept in view that old age and physical decay are synonymous with the shortage of vital substance and faulty functioning of the organs.

1. With this idea in mind, the first advice that Avicenna has given is that mild external and internal lubrication of the old and infirm is very necessary. External lubrication should be done through massage with oil two to three times a day according to

physical weakness, and then a bath should be given depending on the weather.

2. Internal lubrication can be achieved through a diet that has digestible substance. This means that food should be juicy and energy-giving, particularly during the nighttime. Fresh fruits can be given according to taste. Heavy and hard-to-digest foods should be avoided.

3. Avicenna particularly advised that urine and stool should be examined frequently.

4. With regard to exercise, he advised light walking but if this causes weakness, then it is not necessary. Those parts of the body for which movement and exercise are necessary should be ascertained by a physician. It is not good for the old to move all parts.

5. The most invigorating thing for the old is massage, which means manual manipulation of parts of the body (legs, etc.) by rubbing. In fact, in Islamic society the ordinary service of the old means massage, which not only gives them rest but makes them realize their importance.

6. Avicenna has written that during the transition of seasons the dangers of deterioration of old people's health increase. Extra care should therefore be taken. The diet should not only be juicy and pleasant but should not be given in full quantity at a time. It should be given in small quantities at intervals.

These instructions can be carried out in a family system only and that family should be such which has accepted the old and disabled as respectable and worthy of service in the light of Islamic values.

CONCLUSION

In this article I have tried to bring home the fact that the society that Islam wants to establish should be obliging and dutiful. There should be a family system. Because the old have the right of inheritance, it is also their duty to educate and support their children, which has been called as an act of kindness by Islam and has been described as a matter of gratification for the old.

It is the duty of all members of the Society that after meeting their own needs moderately, they should fulfill the rights of the needy, especially the old and disabled. There is a *Hadith* in *Tirmizi* that one of the companions of the Holy Prophet asked, "O Messenger of God, who deserves my care and sympathy more?" The Holy Prophet said, "Mother." He asked thrice and every time the Prophet replied, "Mother." When he asked for the fourth time, the answer came, "Then your Father."

In fact, Islam wants that the spirit of cooperation, compassion, knowledge of good and etiquette should permeate the collective life. Every man of means should become a source of help to his indigent, sick, old and weak neighbor. If a person serves the disabled, he should think that he is doing it as a duty and not as a favor.

In fact, the institutions of charity, inheritance and trust in an Islamic state were meant to protect the indigent, orphans, old and infirm. No wonder, therefore, that such a climate was created in the entire state that no class of people at any stage felt insecure. For Islam has provided a firmer basis than law to fulfill the rights of the needy, the old and the disabled — and that is called piety.

Add Life to Years
the Buddhist Way

Daw Khin Myo Chit

A news item in *Time*, 1970 March 16, featured a picture of the then Secretary-General U Thant prostrating before his 87-year-old mother. The caption runs as follows:

> The formal manners of international diplomacy must have come easily to UN Secretary-General U Thant. A Burmese youth is taught to show respect for parents and elders by prostrating himself when he leaves their presence. And, a son is never too old or too important to kow-tow to his mother, as the 61 year-old statesman demonstrated last week at the Rangoon home of Daw Nan Thuang, 87.

One of the things a small baby learns to do is to clasp its two hands palm to palm and raise them to its forehead in an act of *kadaw*. He does so in humility and with a feeling of gratitude. This act is also a silent apology for any trespasses he might have committed by thought, word, or deed. The seniors do not merely receive the gesture, but they, on their part, ask forgiveness for any wrongful act they may have been guilty of, even if unwittingly. With this reciprocal action of mutual apology, the young and the old can start life afresh; they can start over again with a clean sheet, or as the Burmese say, "erasing the slate," which is synonymous with burying the hatchet.

In Burmese Buddhist society, to be respectful to elders is a strict

---

Permission to publish this material has been granted by the World Health Organization.

religious code and it is also the mark of a well-bred man. Any youngster lacking this manner is regarded as "someone who lacks parental guidance," which is an unflattering reflection on the parents. So, parents usually take pains to teach their young this important tenet taught by the Buddha himself. Young people usually absorb this teaching of being respectful to parents, teachers, and elders through Jataka stories, the stories of the Buddha's former births. Children hear them from their parents or grandparents; they see them illustrated in paintings and sculpture on the pagoda precincts; they see them acted on the stage; they hear them featured in pop songs; and as a recent development, they read them in comic-papers.

THE STORY OF THREE ANIMALS

One well known story is that of the three animals who dwelt near a huge banyan tree in the forest—an elephant, a monkey and a partridge. One day it struck them that it was unseemly to live together without proper respect to one another. They decided to discover who was the oldest among them by asking one another how each first came upon the banyan tree. The elephant said that the tree was only a mere bush when he first saw it and that its topmost branch reached his belly. The monkey said that the tree was only a tiny shoot when he first saw it. The partridge said that there was no tree when he first came to the place; he had eaten the fruits of a banyan tree in a faraway place and voided in this spot, and there grew the tree they now saw. So, the partridge was the oldest; and henceforth the other two, the elephant and the monkey, treated him with due respect. They sought and took counsel whenever needed. The three animals lived with proper ordering of their life by revering and honoring the senior member of the group.

The Buddha taught this story to his disciples to establish the rule of paying respects to the seniors in his Order of Monks. As a preamble to the story, he said:

In the religion I teach, the standard by which precedence in the matter of lodging and the like is to be settled, is not noble birth or having been a Brahman or having been wealthy before the entry into the Order; the standard is not familiarity with the rules of the Order, with the Suttas, or with the Metaphysical books, nor is it either the attainment of any of the four stages of mystic ecstasy, or walking in any of the four paths of salvation.

Brethren, in this religion it is seniority which claims respect of the word, deed and salutation and all the services; it is the seniors who should enjoy the best lodging, the best water, the best rice. This the true standard —

In times past, Brethren, even animals came to the conclusion that it was not proper for them to live without respect and subordination to one another, or without the ordering of their common life —

Titira Jataka: Bk. 1.37

The seniority in the Buddha's Order is counted from the moment one enters the Order and becomes a monk. Seniority of age is the criterion among the lay people, however.

The tradition of being respectful to the seniors teaches the young people courtesy and good manners in their daily behavior. But then, there are certain cultural gaps which often cause "culture shocks" in social encounters with Westerners.

Among the Burmese who are not yet exposed to the ways of the West, the conversation between people who are just introduced starts with the question: "How old are you?" A faux pas, according to the Westerners, but actually a polite gesture showing the willingness to treat the other party with due respect.

The Burmese preoccupation with age and seniority is evident in language; for example, there is no equivalent to the word "brother"; there are two Burmese words, *nyi* (younger brother), *a-ko* (elder brother), but no word for just "brother." This peculiarity once caused an awkward predicament in the Burmese section of the BBC when the news of the Dalai Lama's brother in London was to be on the air. The Program Officer demanded to know whether the man was an elder brother or a younger brother, so that he could render it into Burmese. It so happened that the information was not available; and the Burmese version of the news which was stilted and ridiculous, remained one of the things the BBC man did not like to think of.

The Burmese seldom, if at all — except on occasions that call for strict formality — address a person by name. The epithets, *a-ko-gyi* (big brother), *a-ma-gyi*, (big sister), *u-lay* or *u-gyi* (uncle), *daw daw* or *daw-gyi* (aunt), are used according to the age seniority of the persons involved.

It is seniority, always seniority, that decides how a well-bred person addresses and speaks to another person. Those who grew up during the pre-war days still remember addressing their teachers of missionary schools as Ma Ma Davis (Miss Davis), or Ma Ma Butt (Miss Butt), "ma ma" being a very affectionate and respectful form for "elder sister." Even today, there are people who remain so Burmese that they do not feel at ease calling their non-Burmese friends by their first name because it means doing without the suffixes Mr., Mrs., or Miss. They often call them *Ko gyi* Joe, or *Ma Ma* Dorothy, et cetera, because they have been taught that this is the polite way of addressing people.

Such customs and manners are more in evidence in places other than Rangoon, where people are more exposed to the ways of the outside. Even there, in the suburban areas, where emigrants from small towns and villages settle, old customs still prevail.

THE BUDDHIST WAY OF LIFE

The Buddhist Way of Life among the lay people is to live according to the tenets laid down in *Sangala Sutta*, a discourse given to a brahman, Sangala by name. The discourse deals with the layman's conduct in daily life and his relationship with his family, teachers, and community. Reciprocal duties between the members of the family are specifically laid down in the discourse. That children should look after their parents in their old age is one of the duties. The Buddha called the parents *Brahma*, a word which denotes the highest and the most sacred in Indian thought.

Next to parents as worthy of reverence come the teachers and elders, relatives and non-relatives alike. Those who do not have parents do not let themselves lack persons for reverence; this is an essential ingredient in a good life, to have ones to revere and respect. (*Second Uruvela Sutta: Anguttra Nikaya catukka Nipata.*) With this teaching in mind, younger senior citizens often play the role of well-bred youths by paying respects to some elder in the clan or in the community; it is one way to feel young and cared for, if "only" spiritually. The tradition of paying respects to elders is a source of spiritual strength.

THE RITUAL OF KA-DAW

Today the ritual of paying respects or *ka-daw* ceremony, is one of the features in school and communal activities. Round about the full-moon day of Thadingyut which falls in October, school children of all ages and sizes take part in the ceremony of paying respects to their teachers. In the community, the elders are the recipients of gifts from the younger members.

For the elders it is a pleasurable experience to be so remembered. And as it happens, the elders of the community are never-failing means of moral support on important social occasions. When a young man wants to make a formal request for a girl's hand, and he has no parents to stand by him, an elderly relative or a senior member of the community is ever ready to substitute. In this way, an elderly person plays an important role in family and communal affairs. Of the vicissitudes of life, old age is often a grim reality of living with a sense of inadequacy and uselessness. When younger people of the family or community show courtesy and respect, and above all, give them a sense of being needed, it certainly tempers the sting of old age.

To Be a Buddhist, If Possible a Burman

Sir George Scott, a British civil serviceman who wrote under the pseudonym of Shwe Yoe, is well known for his deep understanding of the Burmese, and his book *The Burman, His Life and Notions* is still a reliable source of information on Burma. According to Shwe Yoe,

> The best thing a Burman can wish for a good Englishman is that in some future existence, as a result of good works, he may be born a Buddhist and if possible a Burman.

One of the good things about being a Buddhist and a Burman is that one can look forward to the declining years of life with all the blessings which should accompany old age, such as honor, love, obedience and troops of friends. This kind of anticipation has, in these days of materialistic thinking, become a far-off dream in many lands.

In Burmese Buddhist society, the onslaught of materialism is met with the steadfast acceptance of the *Samsara*, the round of rebirths and the working of the Law of Kamma. Burmese Buddhists have their share of human desire for material things of life; to them, however, the attainment of such is not for its own sake, but as a means of support to help them on the long cycle of rebirths until they attain the final goal of *Nibbana*.

A Burmese Buddhist is anxious to do good deeds so that he will be attended by comfort and happiness in all the lives to come as he makes a steady progress along the spiritual path. To be respectful to the elders and parents is one of the best deeds of merit, after the tradition of the noble ones of old, and it is something that can be done with minimum physical effort; it is the spirit that matters.

Young people, like those anywhere, are not always docile. They may question the wisdom of the teaching that the young must be respectful and reverent to the elders, simply by virtue of their years. But then, Buddhist teaching also instructs the elders the proper way to conduct themselves so that they will be worthy of respect and reverence. There are many judicious and forceful admonitions in the Buddha's teachings on this point.

> A man who has learned little grows old like an ox,
> His flesh increase, but not his wisdom.

> Not, therefore, is a man an elder, because his head is grey,
> Though he be ripe for years, yet he is called old in vain.

A man in whom dwell truth, righteousness, non-injury, temperance, and self-control,
He that has rid of himself of faults and is steadfast, that man is
truly called an elder.

Dhammapada

In this way, receiving respects and reverence puts the elders in a
very responsible position. The blessings of old age, have to be
earned by one's own good conduct and practice.

One of the things Buddhism teaches is not to react to people's
frailties with one's own viciousness; in other words, you should not
let the other's imperfections decide your conduct, for then you are
not in command of yourself. Instead of reacting to people's frailties
with one's own viciousness, one should be in control of one's own
actions, as laid down by the wise ones:

One should overcome anger with kindness;
One should overcome evil with good;
One should overcome the niggard with gifts;
And speakers of falsehood with truth.

Dhammapada 223

Communal Activities

Activities in a Burmese Buddhist community in many ways promote amicable relations between the young and the seniors. What
with the year-round festivals and still more festivals in honor of the
local pagodas and family celebrations, all of which have to be done
in the traditional manner, community life is a busy one.

On such occasions, the elders have an important role to play.
They sit over a pot of green tea with the accompaniment of jaggery
sweets and crispies; they give counsel while the young ones do the
"leg work"; they reminisce among themselves, this last activity
being enjoyed most by the young people. There are few things more
interesting than what follows after an elderly person begins a yarn
with, "When I was young — ."

At such gatherings, there persists a mixture of reverence and familiarity, seriousness and levity, propriety and broad humor, when

the older ones are as willing to dig up their questionable pasts as the young ones are eager to listen. If an old gallant is giving the local swains the benefits of his experience, there in another corner his female counterpart is holding court with the sweet young things.

This kind of free and easy relationship between the old and the young coexists with the custom of the young bowing down at the feet of the elders in an act of *ka-daw*. This custom of *ka-daw*, highly placed in the code of conduct, is sometimes a source of somewhat unseemly jokes. For example, this is how a man commented on the toughness of meat, an item on the menu when he had a rice meal in a friend's house. "The meat was so tough," he said, "I felt the only thing I should do is to crouch right before the dish and do an act of *ka-daw*; you see, the animal must be my senior by years."

It shows how deeply the tradition of paying respects to the elders is rooted in the minds of the people.

A Season of Paying Respects

October, the end of Buddhist lent, is a season for paying respects to elders. It is a festive season with the gloom of monsoon rains giving way to sunny days, and the nights are festooned with illuminations to celebrate the anniversary of the descent of the Buddha from the celestial regions. The Buddha had gone there to see his mother, who had been reborn a celestial. He had made the greatest gift a son could ever make to his mother, the gift of the Dhamma, that would lead to the cessation of all suffering.

Humans, following the tradition begun by the Buddha himself, establish the season as one for paying respects to parents and elders. It is a happy time for all; young people in their best holiday finery, and children well-scrubbed and well-dressed, almost unfamiliar in their uncommonly good behavior, walk the streets amidst the festivities and open-air stage shows. They must pass by the fun spots until they have performed the act of *ka-daw* to their elders.

Older folks keep open house and they have small change to distribute among the children. It is easy to treat the young guests with snacks, because it usually happens that one group of youths is followed by another, and so whatever cakes and fruits the previous group has brought and presented to the host is the bill-of-fare for the next group. And it goes on and on throughout the season.

October is also a month for weddings, which are considered unlucky during lent, the period of three rainy months. Newly married couples, beautiful people in their first flush of happiness, do their rounds of visits to elders and pay their respects; this way they start their married life with the goodwill and blessing of the elders.

Thingyan Water Festival: New Year

During the three-day Thingyan water festival, which welcomes the new year, the ritual of *ka-daw* is performed as a matter of course. Young people go round with goblets of scented water and traditional shampoo, a brew of boiled soap, acacia fruits and strips of bark from the linden tree, which gives a cool effervescent effect. For needy old folks there will be gifts of new clothes and useful things like soap, towels and medicine. Such times are fun; young ones tease one another and argue noisily never agreeing how things should be done; as they potter around to do the chores, some fetch water, some grind *thanakha* bark on the circular stone slab to make paste, a cooling "face-pack" and talcum for the body; of course, there is more noise and talk than work, but no one minds, least of all the old folks, who are happy enough to have the young ones around them. Older folks recollect the times when they as youngsters performed the same ritual for the "old ones" of their day. The young ones, even as they listen to the yarns, studded with incidents of youthful pranks and peccadilloes, cannot but be reminded of the inevitability of old age. The old ones they see today were youngsters once, and they too shall grow old.

As it happens, paying respects to parents and elders is one way of preparing the young for the years to come, the years of growing old gracefully. As young people learn to extend their sympathy to the old, loving kindness, thoughtful attention, and patience come easily. It is no wonder, then, that "generation gap" is a strange and unfamiliar expression in this part of the world.

One Jataka story tells of a parrot, the leader of the flock, who practiced this principle of caring for parents and the aged.

Once upon a time, there was a huge parrot, leader of a flock who fed on paddy grains. The leader parrot, after eating his fill, always took away a large quantity of sheaves laden with grain.

The farm watchman tried to drive away the flock, but there were too many; he was both annoyed and intrigued by the way the leader parrot carried away the grains in his beak. One day, he set a snare of horse hair and caught the leader bird.

Even as the snare caught his feet, the leader bird forbore to cry out until his flock had had its fill of grains and flown away in safety. The watchman noticed that, so he thought it judicious to take the bird to his master, Kosiya, the brahman. The conversation between the parrot and the brahman is as follows.

The brahman said:

> the bellies of all bellies are out-bellied by you; first a full
>   meal, then off you fly with a good beakful too!
> Have you a granary to fill? or do you hate me sore? I ask of
>   you, come tell me true — where do you put your store?!

The parrot king answered:

> I hate thee not, O Kosiya; no granary I won; Once in my
>   wood I pay a debt and also grant a loan, and there I store
>   treasure up; so be my answer known

The brahman asked:

> What is the loan which you grant? what is the debt you pay?
> Tell me the treasure you store up and fly free away.

The parrot king answered:

> My sallow chicks, my tender brood, whose wings are still
>   ungrown,
> Who shall support me by and bye; to them I grant the loan.
> Then my own ancient parents, who far from youth's hounds
>   are set
> With that within my beak I bring to them I pay my debt.
>   And those birds of helpless wing and weak full many
>   more,

To these I give in charity this sages call my store
This is that loan which I grant, this is the debt I pay
And this the treasure I store up, now I have said my say.

The brahman, pleased with what heard, said:

What noble principles of life! how blessed is the bird.
From many men who lived on earth such rules never heard
Eat, eat your fill whereas you will, with all your kindred
    too;
And parrot, let us meet again, I love the sight of you.

With these words, the brahman looked upon the parrot with a soft heart as though it were his own son; and loosing the bonds from its feet, he rubbed them with oil and fed him out of a golden dish and offered a thousand acres of rice fields for the use of the parrot and his flock. The parrot declined the thousand acres of fields but took only eight acres for his flock. The brahman set up boundary stones and made over the property to the parrot. The parrot went home to his sorrowing parents and his flock, who were happy to welcome him back. They were even happier when the parrot told him of the gift the brahman had made.

Salikedara-Jataka, Pakinnaka-Nipata

MAKING THE MOST OF LIFE—THE BUDDHIST WAY

Burmese Buddhists, with their steadfast acceptance of *samsara*, the round of rebirths and the Law of Kamma, feel it unwise to attach too much importance to what they can get out of their present life. For what does a life span of eighty or even a hundred years matter against an infinity of rebirths, a long way to go until they attain *Nibbana*?

In their later years, when they feel "time's winged chariot hurrying near," they do not try to run that unequal race by trying to grab and devour like amorous birds of prey, all the good things life has to offer, because they do not see the future after death as "vast deserts of eternity." They have to think of things that would accompany them on their long journey in the cycle of rebirth. Even in their younger and more active years, their "lust for life" has always been harnessed and channeled to the mindfulness of the future lives to come. The ever-present concern to do good deeds that would be their stay and support on their long journey, becomes more and more urgent and important in their later years.

In their old age they are more and more anxious to do various kinds of meritorious deeds. If they do not have enough means to build a pagoda or a monastery, they can contribute towards such works, a contribution in cash, no matter how small, is in order; and one can contribute manual labor like carrying bricks. In this way, Burmese Buddhists, instead of trying to make the most of this present short life by trying to acquire material things, do good deeds. And one of them is to give sons into the Buddha's Order of *Buddha Sasana*, that is, to novitiate them. This is one act which no Burmese Buddhist wants to miss.

A NEW LEASE ON LIFE

A man's life is not considered perfect and well lived until and unless he has worn the Buddha's robe and stayed in the monastery for a time. Boys are sent to the monastery and placed under a senior monk who invests them with the robes and gives instructions on living a religious life. They stay as long as they can, usually a week or more, and come back to lay life to pursue their education or training. Again at twenty a Buddhist may enter the monastery and this time be ordained a full member of the Order, a *thera* (monk), a crowning moment in a man's life.

Novitiation, as well as ordination, is a two way meritorious deed, benefiting both the one who is novitiated or ordained, and the one who donates the expenses of the ceremony. For parents it is the greatest gift they can confer on their sons. Parents are anxious to novitiate their sons as soon as the boys are old enough to manage the robes and bear to stay in the monastery, usually about seven.

Novitiation is a joyful family occasion when relatives and neighbors help towards the success of the ceremony. It is also important in the life of the elders. They look forward to seeing their grandsons novitiated, and if possible contribute towards the ceremony. It is a happy family who is able to novitiate the boys while the grandparents are well and alive.

The elders look forward to seeing their grandsons novitiated and they hope to be still around when the boys are twenty and old enough to be ordained. Perhaps, with luck, they may even see their great-grandchildren novitiated. Such hopes and expectations can give the elders a new lease on life, and add life to their years.

Monasteries: Refuge for the Old

Living and growing old in the Buddhist way, it is natural for the elders to take refuge in the monastery. There is a saying, "When a Burman grows old, to some quiet corner of a monastery he goes." It is quite common for some irascible elder, who is no longer amused by the antics of the young, to say, "One of these days, I will go into a monastery."

This is not mere ranting. When an elder says these words, he has perfect confidence and faith that the monastery, the shrine of the Buddha's Dhamma, will offer him solace and comfort and above all, peace and quiet, that he could never hope to have in a householder's life.

Elders of the Buddha's Time: Upaka

Elders of the Buddha's time had, in the same way, taken refuge in the Buddha. The first on record is Upaka, the ascetic, who was the first man to see the Buddha on the very day of his attaining Enlightenment. The Buddha was on his way to the Deer Park, where he was to deliver his first sermon, Dhammacacca, to the five disciples.

Upaka was struck by the beauty of the Buddha's person and the serenity of his appearance, so he asked, "Who are you?" The Buddha answered, "I am Jina" (Conqueror). Upaka mused over the Buddha's answer and went on his way, directly, opposite to where the Buddha was going, but he never forgot the Buddha's words.

It is ironical that Upaka, who was the first person to see the Buddha on the day of his Enlightenment, did not get the fruits of the Buddha's Dhamma then and there. His fruition had to wait until the ascetic had gone through the woes of life, which he never once thought he would have.

After Upaka parted ways with the Buddha, he met a hunter in the forest. The hunter became his disciple and gave him a hut to live in with all the amenities of food and robes. One day when the hunter was on his hunting trip, he left the task of sending food to Upaka to his daughter, Capa. When Upaka saw Capa, he fell madly in love with her. Upaka became sick and almost died from his desire for Capa, so the hunter gave her to him in marriage. Soon they had a son. Now, Upaka, old and unprepossessing, ignorant of the responsibilities of a householder's life, was despised by his young wife. Old and useless, he was mocked and insulted every day. When the child cried, Capa would say, "Don't cry, ascetic's son." At last, he could no longer take his wife's scornful treatment. He bridled in anger and said, "Capa, don't you think for a moment that I, just because I have been a wandering ascetic, do not have friends to stand by me. I do have a friend. He is Jina and to him I will go." So saying, in spite of Capa's entreaties not to leave her and the child, he went away looking for Jina, his friend.

Now the Buddha in his omniscient wisdom saw Upaka's coming. So, he said to his disciples, "A man shall come today asking, 'Where is Jina?' Bring him to me." Soon, Upaka came asking everyone he met, "Where is Jina?" He was duly brought to the Buddha's presence.

Upaka greeted the Buddha, "Exalted one, dost thou know me?" The Buddha answered, "Yes, I know thee. But, where hast thou spent the time?" Upaka told the Buddha what had happened to him. The Buddha asked Upaka, "Thou art now an old man. Can't thou bear religious life?"

Upaka said he could indeed bear religious life, old though he was. So he was ordained and taught the eight-fold noble path. He followed the path diligently, and soon he attained the highest stage of enlightenment, *Arahatship*.

It all goes to show that one is never too old nor too late to take refuge in religion. Upaka's story is a favorite of playwrights and poets; it is represented on the stage, more often than not in burlesque form. The story is also seen in paintings and sculptures on the precincts of pagodas. Stories of men and women of the Buddha's time, who in their extremity of old age took refuge in the Buddha's teaching, are never dated. Their plight of loneliness, helplessness and misery is timeless, as in the case of Lady Sona.

Lady Sona, Wife of a Rich Clansman

Sona was the wife of a rich and noble clansman and she bore him ten sons and daughters. Her husband left the world to enter the Buddha's Order. He left her richly endowed, but she unwisely gave all her property to her ten children, leaving nothing for herself. She hoped that her children would support her in her old age.

It was not long before she realized the injudiciousness of her action. She no longer had means of her own and not one of her ten children gave her due respect, let alone support. She decided then to follow her husband's way and enter the Buddha's Order of Bhik-khunis (nuns).

Sona realized her adversity: she had come late into the Order; she was old and weak; as a junior member of the Order she had to bear the burden of manual labor around the nunnery. If she were to achieve enlightenment, the only meaningful thing in entering the Order, she would have to be more strenuous in effort than others. This she resolved to do.

Since she had no time to practice during the day, she denied herself sleep and practiced at night — "steadfast and unfalteringly as one might cling to a pillar on a veranda or a tree in the dark, for fear of hitting one's head on obstacles, never letting go."

The Buddha in his omniscient wisdom saw Sona maturing in her practice, so he appeared to her in all his glory and said:

> The man who, living for a hundred years,
> Beholdeth never the ambrosial path
> Had better live no longer than one day,
> So, he behold within that day, that path.

Sona, comforted and inspired by the Buddha's words, attained the highest stage of enlightenment, Arahatship. Later, the Buddha honored her among the congregations of gods and men as "one who is first and foremost in capacity for strenuous effort."

Today, as in the Buddha's time, his teaching is still a solace and comfort to many in their affliction of old age and helplessness. Taking refuge in the monastery is not only satisfying spiritually but also a practical thing to do.

When old age comes upon people, they often look for something to hold on to—something that will accompany them on the heavy journey in their declining years. At such times, children, worldly goods, even at their best, do not fulfill the need for a satisfying and contented life. At such times, retiring into a monastery is often the best answer for the Burmese Buddhist—even if it is only for a short time. Elders find occasional retreats helpful to their physical and spiritual well being and what is more, they acquire more equanimity in living with the younger generation.

Monasteries, thanks to the generosity of the donors, are usually spacious and comfortable; there are rest houses for lay people who wish to stay there to practice or study the Buddha's Dhamma. Retiring into the monastery does not necessarily mean that one becomes a monk or a nun; and the stay can be as long or as short as you like.

Some elders coming to stay in the monastery may have means of their own, but there are others who are not so fortunate. Those who come and stay in the monastery out of sheer necessity become virtually dependents of the monastery. There is usually plenty of food, thanks to the donors, and the feeding of the dependents is no problem at all. There is no dearth of helpers who gladly contribute creature comforts for the elders, especially during the season of "paying respects."

Lay people living in the monastery have to observe certain rules. There are regulations laid down for the relationship between the lay residents and the monks. According to the rules of the Order, a monk cannot offer a lay man food, unless the latter is one who either practices or studies the Dhamma, or who does some service in the form of chores for the monastery.

The elders, knowing the rules and obligations, perform chores round the monastery as much as their strength and health permit. There is so much to do around the monastery: sweeping and weeding the grounds, watering the plants and least of all, waiting on the monks as they take their meals. In this way, old people often find life in the monastery more active, healthy and satisfying than living with son's or daughter's families, however, much they may be able and willing to support them.

But this contentment and sufficiency cannot be acquired without the years of closeness and intimacy with the religious teachers and places of retreat. One might find religion cold comfort and monasteries strange and forbidding, without the years of preparation at various stages of one's life. The calm trust and reliance on the monasteries and monks cannot be called upon only at the hour of need. Buddhists have had their religious fervor cultivated all through their years; its strength is their stay and refuge in their old age. They have known monasteries as places of blameless enjoyment in their younger days; they have played on the grounds even while they were doing the jobs of sweeping or weeding. There has also been an expectation of appreciation for their small services, namely sweets and snacks. All this and a promise of happiness hereafter, too!

In their old age, Burmese Buddhists find monasteries open to them with the promise of cordiality and loving kindness and compassion. The strength of religious faith they have built up since their younger days becomes the pillar of strength in their hour of need.

Taking refuge in the monastery — taking refuge in religion — is not regarded in Burmese Buddhist society as the last resort of a man in dotage or of one who has prematurely found himself out of circulation as a social failure. Instead, it is a happy, peaceful and satisfying phase of one's life, something anyone can achieve.

Monasteries, to this present day, are still places of refuge for the old, but the question is how long this can go on in the face of economic stress and other problems of modern living. Especially in large towns and cities, the need for some organized help for the old becomes more and more of a necessity.

CARING FOR THE ELDERS: HOMES FOR THE AGED

Burmese society is close-knit, as all agrarian societies are. What is known as "neighborly help" virtually takes care of many of the social problems in the provincial areas today. The need for organized help was hardly, if at all, felt until quite recently.

The tradition of neighborly help is in itself a form of *dana*, the basic tenet of Buddhist teaching. One begins to be a good Buddhist by first practicing *dana*. The conventional way is to build shrines and establish monasteries and to support the cause of Buddhism by supplying the four requisites: namely alms, food, places of abode, robes and medicines to the monks, who are the bearers of the torch of Buddhist learning.

The practice of *dana*, however, is also the support and mainstay of Old People's Homes. In this way, care for the aged becomes both a religious duty and a social obligation. Religious teaching, cultural tradition and social conscience all merge together to help the elders to lead a contented and useful life. At present, homes for the aged are established in large towns by voluntary organizations, and they are given aid by the State.

The first Home for the Aged and the Sick on record was established in 1864 at Mandalay under the patronage of King Mindon. After the British annexation, however, the homes just faded away, and except for a rare old manuscript showing the city plan of Mandalay with the sites of the homes for the aged and sick, with staff quarters properly attached, no one seemed to have remembered the existence of such institutions.

In 1916, a home for the aged was established at Mingun, a small town on the side of the Irrawaddy River opposite Mandalay. Mingun is well known for its huge unfinished pagoda and great bell. The founding of the home, though well understood as an act of *dana* was rather on the unbeaten track, and it was a solo performance by an enterprising spinster, Daw Oo Zun. She was born in 1868, during the time of King Mindon. Her parents were rich silk merchants. Losing her parents in 1890, while still in her teens, Daw Oo Zun became the head of the silk business, which prospered under her management. She was able to establish a large monastery, an academy of Buddhist learning, under a learned monk.

In 1914, Daw Oo Zun went on a pilgrimage to famous shrines and temples, including the Shwedagon pagoda in Rangoon. She visited the home for the aged run by the Catholic missionaries. There she saw that the elders were given all the comfort and care they needed. But what moved Daw Oo Zun was that most of the elders, who were Buddhist by birth and faith, could not do their daily ritual of taking refuge in the three gems, the Buddha, the

Dhamma and the Sangha. Instead, they had to do the Christian worship rituals.

Even while appreciating the good work done by the missionaries, Daw Oo Zun could not but be distressed by the plight of the Buddhist elders, who were denied the practice of the Buddha's teaching in their last years, the worst possible thing that could happen to a Buddhist. There should be a home run the Buddhist way, she decided.

Daw Oo Zun was determined to establish a home for elders. As soon as she returned from her travels, she took steps to make her dream come true. She conferred with a venerable monk who resided at Mingun and sought his counsel. The monk advised her to use the space between the Great Bell and the unfinished pagoda.

Immediately, Daw Oo Zun had the place cleared of the bushes and three small buildings built, two to house the elders and one for her and her maid, all at her own expense. By 1916, she had three clients, one old man, aged 95, and two women, aged 96 and 85.

Daw Oo Zun personally looked after the elders; she did the cooking herself and fed them with her own hands. Most important of all, the elders were given facilities to practice their daily devotions. Once a week, on every sabbath day, a venerable monk came and invested them with the simple ritual of the three gems, a confirmation of their faith.

Two years later, the number of inmates grew to twenty, and the Eng Ang Tong Pharmacy of Tiger Brand medicines contributed medicines for the home. Letters requesting accommodation for elders came from all parts of the country. Daw Oo Zun called a meeting of helpers and sympathizers at her residence at Mandalay and a Board of Trustees was formed for the management and maintenance of the home. From then on the work expanded, and electricity and running water were installed at the home. The interest of the people was aroused, and pilgrims to the Mingun pagoda and the Great Bell made it a point to visit the home. Daw Oo Zun maintained a motor launch of a hundred-passenger capacity to give free trips to pilgrims from Mandalay to Mingun.

People were awakened to the need for organized help for the elders, and Daw Oo Zun's generosity and selfless dedication became an inspiration. Not only that, a new way of practicing *dana* was opened out for the Burmese Buddhists, who were reminded of the words in the Buddha's discourses:

He who wishes to serve and attend on the Buddha,
Such a one should serve and attend on the sick and the aged.

These lines are today highlighted on the brochures of the homes.

Contributions poured in, and by the 1920s, extensions were added to the home. Requests to establish homes in other towns came, and in 1927, a home was established in Thaton; in Rangoon in 1929, and in Pakokku in 1932. In 1928, Daw Oo Zun then 60 years old, became a nun, giving away her cache of jewelry worth the current price of 200,000 rupees to the cause of the homes and spent the last years of her life in the service of the elders. She died at Mingun in 1944.

Today the homes are maintained and expanded. Daw Oo Zun's name is affectionately remembered as a pioneer in this field of social services. Her indomitable energy and dedication to the caring of the elders had become a legend even in her own life-time. Last, but by no means least, her courage that enabled her to give away her worldly goods and to live a life of voluntary poverty became a shining example of the Buddha's teaching: "The essence of worldly goods that are forever open to the perils of floods, fires, thieves, kings and personal enemies, is in the renouncing of them."

The spirit of *dana* in the Buddhist teaching is essentially renunciation; in giving something away, one automatically cuts the attachment to the thing given away; the final goal of *nibbana* is the stage of enlightenment, when one has cut away all forms of attachment. A Buddhist prepares himself for the goal by first starting to cut the attachment to things he can give away, however small. In this way, the practice of *dana* puts a Buddhist on the road to *nibbana*; therefore, Buddhists of all levels of wealth, intellect and station in life are anxious to begin with acts of giving. Thus, it is not too difficult to run charitable institutions.

There is a Burmese saying: "If you do not know how to practice *dana*, go and be a vendor in the market place." For those not familiar with the ways of the Burmese, who have their share of idiosyncrasies, the meaning might be obscure. In this part of the world, when a customer buys something, she expects the vendor to give her *ah-sit*, which is a small "extra" added to the things already bought. (This custom is just the reverse of a customer giving tips to the vendor or the salesman for whatever services she has received.) *Ah-sit* is often the bone of contention between the customer and the vendor, especially when the former is unduly insistent on her demand for what she thinks to be her right. Most vendors are willing to give *ah-sit*, to add a little extra something to wares like fish, meat, vegetables or groceries. When the customer says that she is shopping for an alms-giving, that is offering alms food to monks, the vendor is glad to contribute something so that she gains a share of the merit, even while she is doing the mundane business of making a living. However, it would be the worst possible taste on the part of the customer to demand an *ah-sit* just because she is going to have an alms-giving. She can mention this only out of loving kindness to give the vendor a chance of gaining merit.

This spirit of *dana* is evident in the fiscal reports of the homes for the aged. Among the donors of the daily food for the inmates of the home are the names of the local vendors, who donate their wares, like meat, fish, vegetables, fruits and groceries on weekly or monthly basis.

Dana is the mainstay of all activities in the community. It is quite impossible to do anything without distributing gifts, however small. There is a tradition, today rarely seen in cities, but still in practice in provincial areas; when a family announces an event, happy or sad, or passes invitations to an alms-giving, it is done with an offering of a small gift such as a packet of picked tea or cheroots. Guests come with gifts, usually as contribution to the offerings to monks, and the host has "take-away-gifts" ready for friends who are kind enough to come. Take-away-gifts could be small, such as a packet of jaggery sweets, or fancy things such as lacquer goblets, trays, napkins, depending on the means of the host. In this way, giving comes easy to Burmese Buddhists, whatever their station in life, and the traditional habit of openhandedness is a considerable help in the running of homes. Burmese Buddhists celebrate their anniversaries by giving *dana*, usually offering alms-food to monks, but these are also occasions for giving donations to the homes. The reports of the homes for the aged often include the names of the donors who contribute cash or kind on their birthdays or on the anniversary of their parents' passing away.

The Burmese do not just throw a party on a happy anniversary; there is always some serious purpose, like remembering the old helpless ones in the homes. Friends come to rejoice in the good deeds done for the day and "gain a share." According to Buddhist teaching, anyone who rejoices in the good deeds done by others gains a share of the merit. The donor who shares the merit of his deed with others does not lose any part of his own merit, for a deed of merit is as boundless as the sea and the more he shares with others, the more he gains.

Sharing one's good deeds with others often gives "culture shocks" because, according to the code of manners of the West, one does not "boast" of one's good deeds; one does them on the quiet. Here, the writer would like to say something from experience.

One afternoon I was having tea with the wife of a resident diplomat here in Rangoon. She had some house guests from her home country. As we were having small talk, my hostess drew my attention to the old butler who was serving us. She said that the man had been deaf for over twenty years. Some time ago, a specialist from her home country came, so she put him under his care and had him operated on; now he could hear. Knowing that my hostess was conversant with our ways and customs, I thanked her for sharing the good deed with me and said, "Well done," three times, the usual response Buddhists make when someone shares his good deed. My hostess then turned to her house guests and said that she could never have told anyone in her home country what she had told me just now. Here in Burma, it is a beautiful gesture of warmth and loving kindness showing the willingness to share the merit of a good deed with friends.

The homes often publish occasional "house magazines," which make interesting reading. They are not merely factual reports. The professional writers who cover the various aspects of the homes write with special warmth and humanity, and more often than not, their account of the selfless dedication of the staff is tempered with a sense of deep humility. The thumb nail sketches of the inmates and staff members alike are poignant as well as inspiring. Nurses and workers often express satisfaction in their work, which fulfills their emotional and spiritual needs to take care of the elders who stand in for parents long passed away.

A TRANQUIL LIFE AFTER CROWDED YEARS

In 1969, a reporter for the house magazine interviewed a most unlikely inmate of a home for the aged in Rangoon. U Su of Prome was not a mere man, but an institution, a grand hulk of a man who had weathered the storms that had raged over the country while her history was being made during the years of anti-colonial movement of the 1920s.

U Su, born of rich family, was a high school student when he got involved in the Students' Boycott of 1920 that triggered off a national awakening of considerable strength and far-reaching effects. He spent his youthful years in India, Ceylon, and later in Germany, taking courses in industrial business management. The means of his family could only be surmised from the fact that it supported him during his seven years abroad and later when he participated in the political activities after his return in 1927.

Young, rich, and debonair, enhanced by the worldly sophistication the years abroad had given him, U Su became a luminary in the political scene. He became the Secretary of the General Council of Buddhist Associations in Burma, the national front of political movement, and later rose to head the organization, was privileged to bear the prestigious title of "President," which is synonymous with "Uncrowned King." In 1930, he was one of the organizers of the peasants' revolt. He went to Delhi as one of the members of the mission invited by the Viceroy of India on the question of Separation of Burma from India. He also attended a conference of statesmen in London in 1931.

So, U Su, a political activist, rebel, diplomat, the founder and organizer of various associations, a writer of political and religious books, and a newspaper columnist, was now sitting calmly in the parlor of the home for the aged. In spite of his years, he carried his tall frame with poise and dignity. There was an aura of reserve, though he looked genial and amiable.

"No use talking of the days that are no more," U Su said. "I always contemplate on these stanzas (of the venerable Tut Khaung Sayadaw), simple and easy to remember, 'Young, fresh and handsome, one ends up old and shriveled.'"

He smiled, perhaps remembering for a moment his youthful days. "Happy and rapturous with loved ones, it ends in the anguish of parting. Rising high to glorious heights, one ends in an ignominious fall." Here he chuckled good naturedly remarking how he was lionized in those days, and then what a fall there was! When he came to the stanza, "Being endowed with worldly goods, one ends up in poverty and humiliation," U Su smiled and said, "I had had more than my share of that experience of being courted and flattered because of my wealth and position, and later—this—all alone and deserted." He said the last words with the cheerful grin of a man who had never been beguiled by fickle fortune and so had known that this would be the end. After making shrewd observations on the truth of the Buddha's teaching expressed in the stanzas, he said; "All these I have found to be true, but," here again he smiled roguishly, "I have not had the experience of the last stanza—yet—it says, 'Being alive and well, one ends up in death,' but I know it will be true, too."

This man who had lived a full, active, and important life had found peace and tranquility in the Buddha's teaching. He waited for death not with fear but with calmness.

A Prima Donna

In *Add Life to Years*, an anthology of writings by professional writers, active social workers and practicing doctors, which has recently been published by the Ministry of Health, an article by Kanbawza Myint Lwin tells of his meeting with Ma Sein Hmon (Miss Diamond Dust), a well-known prima donna now in her eighties, at the Home for the Aged in Mandalay.

Miss Diamond Dust came into the parlor tapping her staff softly on the floor. Still incredibly lithe and slim, she moved with exquisite grace. She peered at me through her horn rimmed spectacles and a ghost of a smile hung on her lips. She greeted me benignly, and as she spoke, her finely chiseled face became alive, and I suddenly realized what charm, what allure, must have enthralled our grandfathers, the then ardent swains of those days.

At my request, she crooned a song, a lyric in praise of the beauty of the country around the Mandalay hill. The song rose to sublime heights as it echoed the peace and tranquility of the Buddhist shrines around. It was indeed a happy turn of fate that Miss Diamond Dust found her refuge there in her declining years.

She was born of a farmer's family in a village near Rangoon; at an early age she began hoofing and singing on the local stage during the seasonal festivals. Her talent bloomed under the guidance and training of a master marioneteer. He was a manipulator of a male dancer puppet, so her steps were more on the springy side. With her natural grace and femininity, her performance had the elfin charm of a tomboy and it delighted the audience all the more.

In doing the classical dance steps one ability of a prima donna is to manage the long white train of her sarong, a demonstration of skill as well as art — a virtuoso performance and no less. Miss Diamond Dust, uncommonly adroit in this particular act, once used it to put an overly arduous swain in his place. He was the son of a rich landowner, and he once had her troupe perform on the grounds of his home for his private entertainment.

Miss Diamond Dust who had so long been pestered by his unwelcome attentions, was determined to have her revenge. She sang and tripped along the extreme edge of the stage, where the enraptured young man sat. As the music heaved and rolled down to a triumphant close, she gave a dexterous kick with her light fantastic toe so that the train of her sarong flowed and whirled, slapping the young man's face, which for some moments was entirely enveloped in the voluminous folds of the long flowing train. In a society where cultural tradition rules that no man walks under the clothesline on which woman's skirts are hung except at the risk of having his male mystique destroyed, the humiliation was complete.

Her eyes twinkled as she recounted her youthful prank. It could be surmised that stage was her one and only love of her life. She spoke of her short married life and its break-up without bitterness or self pity, but with humor and a pretty wit that betrayed no sense of regret.

She was still in good health, and all her long life she had hardly had any serious problems. She had worked well into her fifties and she had never known fatigue. She had not taken the flesh of quadrupeda since she was thirty, which left her diet of vegetables and other things only sparingly. She said that the diet was conducive to mental peace and tranquility. It helped her to be moderate in her passions — greed, anger and envy. Above all, the diet kept her physique trim and supple. She used to smoke Burmese cheroots but she had given them up quite recently. In her performing days she could do with very little sleep. In spite of the ungodly hours her profession demanded, she hardly ever took a nap during the day. Now, in her retirement, her hours were more regular. She said that she spent her time now in meditation and contemplation, and of course, here her eyes twinkled mischievously, "in reminiscing with fellow inmates of the home," who were only too willing to be fascinated by the magic that was hers.

WHAT WRITERS IN THEIR SEVENTIES SAY

Add Life to Years also includes articles by writers in their seventies. They have some interesting things to say about diet and health. Some elders often have their own very individual way of treating their physical ills. The cures are unpredictable and often unconventional. U San Ngwe, a writer, scholar, and researcher in his seventies gives a recipe for a healthy old age, which includes mental strength and the tenacity to go on working. He says:

Do not pollute your mind with vapors of greed, anger, envy and resentment; do not let other peoples' affairs get into your head. Whenever I feel worried, or annoyed, or depressed, I just take a book from the shelf — any book — and open any page and read it. The first five lines may not do me any good, but by the time I get to ten, fifteen lines, then twenty, all my unsavory feelings die away. After that I can hardly remember what I was upset about.

A RECURRING THEME

The traditional custom of paying respects to elders and the extended family system is a recurring theme in the discussion on the care of elders. In some countries, attempts are being made to revive old customs and some are going so far as to make laws to force people to take care of their parents in old age. With this new trend in the handling of social problems, it is pertinent to quote a story from the *Dhammapada*.

The Old Brahman and His Four Sons

Once, during the lifetime of the Buddha, there lived in the city of Savatthi a rich Brahman. He had four sons, and when they married he divided half of his wealth among them, keeping the other half for himself. Later, his wife died and the sons feared that he might take another wife and start a new family. This would mean that they would not be able to enjoy the rest of the wealth, still in the Brahman's hands. So, the sons persuaded the old Brahman to divide the remainder of his wealth among them; after all, they said, they would all minister to his needs. So the old Brahman gave the rest of his wealth to his sons, keeping only the clothes he had on his back.

He first stayed with his eldest son, who attended on him well — but only for some short time. It was not long before the daughter-in-law began nagging him: Why should he be living with them all the time? Other sons also had an equal share of inheritance; why should they not share the responsibility of taking care of the old father?

So the old man went and stayed with the second son, where the same thing happened within a short time. He went from one son to another until he had no place to go. Having no roof over his head, and no means of support, he became a mendicant in one of the non-Buddhist sects. After months of near starvation, he became ragged and worn out. When he looked for help and comfort, he could think of no one but the Buddha; he said to himself, "They say that the monk Gautama has a countenance that does not frown, a face that is frank and open, that his manner of conversing is pleasant, and that he greets strangers in a kind and friendly way.'' He decided to go to the Buddha.

As he had hoped, the Buddha received him kindly and asked why he, once rich and of high social position, came to be an old ragged mendicant. The Brahman told the whole story. So the Buddha taught the Brahman some stanzas and said: ''Well then, Brahman, when people gather in the hall and your sons and their wives are there together with others, go and recite these stanzas before the company.''

So, on the day when people gathered in the hall, the Brahman's sons and their wives, dressed in fine clothes and bedecked with jewels, sat in the high place as befit their social position. The old Brahman entered the hall and requested the company to hear him recite certain verses. When he was granted permission, he stood up and recited the stanzas the Buddha had taught him.

> They at whose birth I rejoiced, whose birth I desired.
> Even they, instigated by their wives, keep me away as a dog would a hog.
>
> ''Wicked and worthless,'' they say to me, ''Dear Father, Dear Father.'' Ogres in the form of sons, they forsake me in my old age.
>
> When a horse is grown old and useless, he is deprived of food; So likewise a father of simpletons, as a monk, begs his food from door to door.
>
> Better the staff for me than disobedient sons; The staff keeps off the savage bull and likewise the savage dog.
>
> In darkness he was before; in the deep shallow prospers.
>
> By the power of the staff he recovers his footing when he stumbles.

Now, at that time this was the law of mankind: ''If any devour the sustenance of mother and father, he shall be put to death.'' The sons of the Brahman fell at their father's feet and begged him to spare their lives. Out of the softness of a father's heart, the Brahman asked the people to spare his sons who would support and attend to him in the future.

Thoroughly admonished, the sons took the old Brahman home, carrying him on a chair borne by themselves. At home he was bathed and anointed with scented oils, and choicest food was placed before him. He lay down on the soft bed prepared for him and fell asleep.

When he woke up refreshed and strong, he realized how much he owed the Buddha for his present state. He took his four sons and their wives to the Buddha, and hearing the Buddha speak the Dhamma, they all were established in the right path and to the end of their lives they lived accordingly.

Dhammapada Book 23: Naga Vagga, Story No. 3

The story of the four undutiful sons convicted of the failure of filial duty and facing the extreme penalty might seem incongruous in these "civilized times." But, then, with the daily news stories of mass murders, violence, and crimes against humanity flashing over the public media all over the world—perhaps it is not so incongruous after all.

Church Conservatism and Services for the Elderly

Rebecca G. Adams
Bonnie J. Stark

INTRODUCTION

The local church has traditionally provided services to the elderly.[1] During this century, the role of government in human services has grown and partially replaced that of local churches.[2] Recent reductions in government spending on human services, however, have led to a rediscovery of the local church by the service system.[3] Research has focused mainly on the potential for linkages between churches and the social services network.

Although the pastoral care literature includes many discussions of what local churches can or should do for their older members,[4] there have been very few studies of what churches have been doing for them. There are three notable exceptions. Cook[5] surveyed 111 local, regional, and national religious organizations, representing a constituency of 262,766 congregations. He identified 52 types of

Rebecca G. Adams is Assistant Professor of Sociology and Chair of the Gerontology Program Committee at the University of North Carolina at Greensboro. Bonnie J. Stark is a graduate student in UNCG's Sociology Department. Both can be reached at: Department of Sociology, University of North Carolina at Greensboro, Greensboro, NC 27412.

The data presented in this article were collected through the University of North Carolina at Greensboro Center for Social Research and Human Services. The first of the two surveys was conducted under contract with the Piedmont Triad Council of Governments Area Agency on Aging.

Permission to publish this material has been granted by the World Health Organization.

services provided to the elderly, 42 of which were offered at the local level. The key areas of service were fellowship, social activities, congregational and pastoral ministry, visiting, and recreational activities.

Tobin and Ellor identified 26 types of services offered to older adults by the churches in six Chicago-area communities.[6] Prevalent services included some kind of assistance to participate in church services, counseling, and visitation. Using the same data, Ellor and Coates identified four basic groups of formal and information services: (1) religious programs, (2) pastoral care programs, (3) programs in which the church acted as host to social agency services, and (4) programs in which the church actually provided social services.[7]

Steinitz did in-depth interviews with 42 church clergymen, 40 lay leaders and elderly congregants, and 38 agency personnel and community informants in a suburb of Chicago.[8] Her major findings were that most services provided by churches are organized informally, and there are few linkages between churches and social agencies. Although the authors of all three studies recognized that local churches vary tremendously in their capacity and desire to provide services to older adults. Steinitz was the only one who studied and reported this variation. She found that the proportion of elderly members in the church, congregational size, predominant clerical style, and denominational affiliation all contributed to this variation.

Maves[9] distinguished between the primary and secondary functions of religious groups. The primary functions are spiritual or doctrinal, while the secondary functions involve social action. Congregations vary in conservatism and the tendency for churches to offer social services to older adults. Steinitz[10] reported that churches that were conservative, in the secondary sense, offered fewer services to older adults than those that were not.

The relationship between church conservatism and a tendency not to offer social services to older adults is potentially particularly important in the South. Hill has observed that: "Southern religion perpetuates its tradition of minding the churches' business instead of the society's."[11] If this is a pervasive situation, it may be very difficult for the aging social service network to form links with churches in the southern region.[12]

This article contributes to the research on the potential for linkages between local churches and the aging network in two ways. First, it reports on a study of the services offered to older adults by churches in a southern, primarily rural county. No previous study has focused on this type of population of churches. Second, it addresses the questions of whether there is a relationship between each of the two dimensions of church conservatism and the tendency to offer social services to older adults. Only the secondary or social action dimension has been studied, in this regard, before.

THE DATA

This article is based on data from a 1984-1985 mail survey of the population of churches in Davidson County, North Carolina. The survey was conducted as part of the Davidson County Study on Aging which was a comprehensive needs assessment conducted by the University of North Carolina at Greensboro Center for Social Research and Human Services (CSRHS) under contract with the Piedmont Triad Council of Governments Areas Agency on Aging. In addition to surveying the County's churches, the CSRHS collected data from its 33 community agencies, 2 acute care facilities, and 11 extended care facilities that served older adults and conducted a house-to-house survey of its elderly population.

According to the 1980 Census, Davidson County had 113,162 residents, 14% of whom were 60 years old or older. It includes two cities, Lexington and Thomasville, which had 15,711 and 14,144 residents in 1980, respectively. The remainder of the County is dotted by small towns, but is basically rural. By consulting local religious organizations and telephone books, 222 churches were identified, 21 of which appeared to have folded by the time the study was started.

The mail survey was conducted in two stages. The first questionnaire was initially mailed on November 1, 1984 and included three checklists of services. The pastors indicated which services for older adults their churches offered formally, which services their congregations provided informally, and which services the older adults in their congregations needed. The instrument also included questions about denominational affiliation, the number of members, the number of people usually attending the main service, the percentage of the congregation over the age of 60 years, and staff size. Each questionnaire was accompanied by a letter from the Davidson County Manager and by one from the Director of the CSRHS. Two follow-up letters and additional copies of the questionnaire were sent.

The second stage of the mail survey began on August 12, 1985, when a questionnaire was sent to each of the pastors who had returned the first one. The second questionnaire included questions about the name of the community, the ruralness of the area, the church's organizational affiliations, and the details of the formal services that the pastor had indicated were offered by his or her church. The major focus of the questionnaire, however, was on the religious beliefs and priorities of the congregation. The second stage of the survey was not part of the contracted needs assessment, so the questionnaire was only accompanied by a letter from the Director of the CSRHS. Two follow-up letters and questionnaires were sent and telephone calls were made to non-respondents to encourage them to reply.

Table 1 includes a breakdown of the response rate for each stage of the survey by denomination. Note that all religious organizations in the population were Christian. The response rate for the first stage of the survey was 55.2% (see Table 1, column 3). The response rate for the second stage of the survey was 71.2% (see Table 1, column 5). The overall response rate was thus 39.3% (see Table 1, column 6). The data presented in this article are on the 34.3% of the churches whose pastors answered all of the questions necessary for the analyses (see Table 1, column 8). This response rate is fairly high considering the sensitive nature of the questions included in the second questionnaire. The CSRHS received several letters from pastors who refused to answer the second questionnaire, because they suspected that we were "working for the government" and felt that the government had no business asking questions about religious beliefs.

MEASURES OF FORMAL AND INFORMAL SERVICE PROVISION

When the pastors returned the second questionnaire, it became obvious that many of the services that they had claimed to offer formally were really offered informally. Some of them had kept copies of their original answers and noticed the discrepancy. A few of them included notes such as:

> I am sorry I exaggerated what our church does on the first questionnaire. We do help people get to church on a one-to-one basis, but we don't have an organized program. I wish we did. It is needed.

In other cases, the pastor did not realize that we had only asked them about formal services that they had claimed to provide a scrawled "only informal" or "one-to-one basis" across the page.

The measure of formal service provision presented here is adjusted for these discrepancies. If the pastor could not describe the formal service in the second questionnaire or the description was of an informal service, it was added to his or her list of informal services and deleted from his or her list of formal ones. About 30% of the pastors had described at least one informally provided service as a formally provided one.

MEASURES OF CHURCH CONSERVATISM

The questionnaire was designed to measure church conservatism on both the primary and secondary dimensions.[13] The pastors indicated what proportion of their congregations (all, most, half, fewer than half, none) felt that: (1) if we do not preach Christ to people in other countries who have never heard about Christ, the people in these countries will be damned forever, (2) God always does what you ask God to do in prayer, and (3) the Bible is to be taken literally, word for word. They also rank ordered the importance to their congregations of: (1) prayer and public worship of the Lord, (2) Christian education, (3) evangelism, (4) supporting missions, (5) social action, (6) fostering spiritual growth in members, (7) politi-

TABLE 1

RESPONSE RATES OF CHURCHES BY DENOMINATION

Denomination	1 #in County [a]	2 # Responding to 1st Survey	3 % Response Rate for 1st Survey [b]	4 # Responding to 2nd Survey	5 % Response Rate for 2nd Survey [c]	6 Overall % Response Rate [d]	7 Number in County Responding to Relevant Items	8 % of Number in County Responding to Relevant Items
AME	2	1	50.0	0	0.0	0.0	0	0.0
Assembly of God	2	1	50.0	1	100.0	50.0	1	50.0
Baptist	83	38	45.8	24	63.2	28.9	19	22.9
Catholic	2	2	100.0	2	100.0	100.0	1	50.0
Christian Fellowship	1	0	0.0	0	—	0.0	0	0.0
Christian Missionary Alliance	3	1	33.3	0	0.0	0.0	0	0.0
Church of Christ	2	2	100.0	1	50.0	50.0	1	50.0
Church of God	5	2	40.0	1 [e]	50.0 [e]	20.0 [e]	1 [e]	20.0 [e]
Episcopal	2	2	100.0	2	100.0	100.0	1	50.0
Jehovah's Witness	1	1	100.0	1	100.0	100.0	0	0.0

Denomination								
Lutheran	8	7	87.5	7	100.0	87.5	7	87.5
Methodist	46	24	52.2	19	79.2	41.3	19	41.3
Moravian	1	1	100.0	0	0.0	0.0	0	0.0
Nazarene	1	1	100.0	0	0.0	0.0	0	0.0
Pentecostal	11	5	45.5	2 e	40.0 e	18.2 e	2 e	18.2 e
Presbyterian	6	4	66.7	4	100.0	66.7	4	66.7
Quaker	1	1	100.0	1	100.0	100.0	0	0.0
Seventh Day Adventist	1	1	100.0	0	0.0	0.0	0	0.0
United Church of Christ	16	12	75.0	10	83.3	62.5	10	62.5
Wesleyan	5	5	100.0	4	80.0	80.0	3	60.0
Non-Denomenational	2	0	0.0	0	—	0.0	0	0.0
TOTAL	201	111	55.2	79	71.2	39.3	69	34.3

a Twenty-one additional churches were identified and sent questionnaires, but they were returned as non-forwardable

b Column 2 divided by Column 1

c Column 4 divided by Column 2

d Column 4 divided by Column 1, except see footnote e.

e The second survey was mailed to one church of this denomination and was returned as non-forwardable. Response rate is based on the number deliverable.

f Column 7 divided by Column 1, except see footnote e.

cal action, (8) caring for members' non-spiritual needs, (9) community fellowship among members of the church, and (10) fellowship with other church communities.

RESULTS

Two Dimensions of Church Conservatism

The 13 items designed to measure church conservatism on doctrine and social action were submitted to a confirmatory factor analysis. Six items were eliminated because they had low correlations with other items, their measures of sampling adequacy were low, their communality with other variables was low, or they loaded highly on both factors.

The two-factor results of the final analysis are included in Table 2. A varimax rotation and a maximum likelihood extraction were

TABLE 2

FACTOR LOADINGS FOR BELIEF VARIABLES (N = 69)

Belief Variable	*Factors*	
	Fundamentalism	*Lack of Social Orientation*
Those uninformed of Christ will be damned	0.32	0.05
Literal interpretation of Bible	0.32	-0.06
Evangelism a low priority	-0.60	0.00
God always answers prayers	0.33	-0.04
Political action a low priority	-0.08	0.72
Fellowship among members a low priority	0.08	0.55
Nonspiritual needs of members a low priority	-0.04	0.55

NOTE: Fifty percent of the variance was explained. The eigenvalue for the first factor was 2.01, and eigenvalue for the second factor was 1.95. The two factor solution adequately fit the data (chi-square = 10.4, df = 13, p> 0.66).

used. Bartlett's test of sphericity was significant (p < 0.001), and the Kaiser-Meyer-Olkin measure of sampling adequacy was acceptable (0.71). The eigenvalue for the first factor was 2.01, and the one for the second factor was 1.95. The two-factor model explained 50% of the variance and fit the data (chi-square = 10.4, df = 13, p > 0.66). The variables that loaded relatively highly on each of the independent (i.e. unrelated) factors are underlined. A relatively high loading indicates that a variable was important in defining a factor.

The first factor is a measure of fundamentalism.[14] The congregations of churches with high scores on this dimension felt that those uninformed of Christ will be damned, interpreted the Bible literally, felt that God always answers prayers, and did not consider evangelism as a low priority. The second factor is a measure of a lack of social orientation. The congregations of churches with high scores on this dimension considered political action, fellowship among members, and the non-spiritual needs of members as high priorities.

Formal and Informal Services

Table 3 shows the percentage of churches offering each service, formally, informally, and at least one way. While only 82.6% of the churches offered at least one service formally, almost all of them did so informally (94.2%). The six services churches most often offered formally, in order of decreasing frequency, were: outreach, a social club for older adults, emergency assistance, food distribution, transportation to church, and telephone reassurance. The six services congregation members most often offered informally, in order of decreasing frequency, were: transportation to church, outreach, telephone reassurance, transportation to important appointments, and emergency assistance. The six services most often offered at least one way, in order of decreasing frequency, were: transportation to church, outreach, telephone reassurance, emergency assistance, transportation to important appointments, and information about services.

A few generalizations can be made based on Table 3. First, as Steinitz observed, most of the services offered by the churches were

TABLE 3

PERCENT OF CHURCES OFFERING SERVICES FORMALLY, INFORMALLY, AND FORMALLY AND/OR INFORMALLY (N = 69)

Type of Service [a]	Formally	Informally	Formally and/or Informally
1. Trans. to church	24.6	76.8	82.6
2. Trans. to important appointments	2.9	53.6	53.6
3. Home health care	1.4	7.2	8.6
4. Hospice	10.1	——[b]	10.1
5. Counseling	13.0	——[b]	13.0
6. Outreach	49.3	71.0	81.1
7. Tel. reassurance	20.3	65.2	68.1
8. Senior recreation	13.0	——[b]	13.0
9. Social club for older adults	31.9	——[b]	31.9

	(1)	(2)	(3)
10. Purchasing/preparing food	2.9	17.4	18.8
11. Meal delivery	7.2	—[b]	7.2
12. Food distribuiton	27.5	—[b]	27.5
13. Light housework	2.9	14.5	14.5
14. Heavy housework	1.4	18.8	18.8
15. Reading/letter writing	0.0	10.1	10.1
16. Employment referral	1.4	7.2	7.2
17. Emergency assistance	29.0	49.3	59.4
18. Housing assistance	1.4	8.7	8.7
19. Information about services	14.5	46.4	49.3
At least one	82.6	94.2	95.7

[a] The respondents were also asked about health and nutrition education, adult day care, and congregate meals, but none of the churches offered any of these services, formally or informally. An "other" category was provided, but no respondents made legitimate use of it.

[b] This service is by definition a formal one.

79

organized informally.[15] Second, while the churches often provided services that probably contributed to their primary function (e.g., transportation to church, outreach, and telephone reassurance), they also performed services that one might expect from social service professionals (e.g., transportation to important appointments, emergency assistance, and information about services). Third, services that require special training or access to special resources were rarely offered by churches (e.g., home health care, hospice, counseling, employment referral, meal delivery, and housing assistance).

THE RELATIONSHIP BETWEEN CHURCH CONSERVATISM AND SERVICES OFFERED

Table 4 reports the betas resulting from 106 two-stage regressions. A beta measures the strength of the relationship between variables. Since the scores are standardized, they can be directly compared to one another. For each regression the dependent variable was a measure of whether a church offered a service formally, whether a church offered a service informally, whether a church offered a service at least one way, the total number of formal services offered, or the total number of services offered at least one way. The following variables were entered on the first stage of each regression: number of members, number of persons usually attending the main church service, number of full-time staff equivalents, ruralness of location, and percentage of the congregation over 60 years old. On the second stage of each regression either the factor scores on fundamentalism or the factor scores on lack of social orientation were entered. The betas in the table thus represent the effect of each dimension of church conservatism on each measure of service provision, controlled for the churches' structural characteristics. A negative beta means that the more conservative a church was, the less likely they were to offer the service.

Several generalizations can be made about the results presented in Table 4. First, 27 of the 29 significant betas were positive. In other words, in general, the more conservative the churches were, the less likely they were to offer services to older adults. Second, the fundamentalism dimension was related to the lack of provision of only three services, specifically: hospice, meal delivery, and heavy housework. Third, as one would expect based on Steinitz's work, the total number of services, the total number of informal services, the total number of formal services, and the provision of many specific services were negatively affected by a lack of social orientation.[16]

CONCLUSIONS AND DISCUSSIONS

The data presented here bear on three questions that are related to the general issue of whether linkages between local churches and the social service network are feasible and would make it possible to meet the needs of older adults better. The three questions are: (1) Are the social services offered to older adults by southern rural churches similar to those offered to them by northern urban churches? (2) Has southern religion continued to mind "the churches' business instead of society's"? and (3) Are conservative churches less likely than liberal churches to try to meet the non-spiritual needs of their elderly congregants?

In general, the answer to the first question appears to be a tentative "yes." The services that were offered by the Chicago area churches studied by Steinitz and Robin and Ellor were similar to those offered by the southern, primarily rural churches included in this study.[17] The minor discrepancies are probably the result of the use of different methodologies and instruments. Steinitz developed her categories of service by doing participant observation and conducting unstructured interviews.[18] Tobin and Ellor also did face-to-face interviews, but the categories of their typology of services were different than those used by Steinitz.[19] The Davidson County data were collected through the mail, and, once again, different service categories were used. As Streib has observed, the first step that needs to be taken is the collection of comparable observations.[20] Until this has been done, it will be difficult to compare the results of different studies.

Hill's observations that "southern religion perpetuates its tradition of minding the churches' business instead of society's"[21] appears to be an over-generalization. While it might be true that southern churches are less likely than northern churches to get in-

TABLE 4

BETAS FROM REGRESSIONS OF FUNDAMENTALISM AND LACK OF SOCIAL ORIENTATION FACTORS ON EACH SERVICE TYPE, CONTROLLING FOR # MEMBERS, AVERAGE # ATTENDING MAIN SERVICE, # FULL TIME STAFF EQUIVALENTS, RURAL LOCATION, AND % CONGREGATION 60+

Type of Service	Fundamentalism			Lack of Social Orientation		
	Formal	Informal	Formal and/or Informal	Formal	Informal	Formal and/or Informal
1. Trans. to church	0.10	0.08	0.10	-0.10	0.12	0.06
2. Trans. to important appointments	-0.04	-0.01	-0.12	-0.26 **	-0.12	-0.12
3. Home health care	0.08 *	0.13	0.15	0.08	-0.10	-0.05
4. Hospice	-0.23 *	—b	-0.23 *	-0.15	—b	-0.15
5. Counseling	0.05	—b	0.05	0.09	—b	0.09
6. Outreach	0.05	-0.07	0.01	-0.03	-0.05	-0.13
7. Tel. reassurance	0.06	-0.08	-0.06	-0.34 ***	-0.10	-0.22 *

	(1)	(2)	(3)	(4)	(5)	(6)
8. Senior recreation	0.02	—[b]	0.02	0.02	—[b]	0.07
9. Social club for older adults	0.05	—[b]	0.05	0.05	—[b]	0.23**
10. Purchasing/preparing food	0.09	-0.03	0.05	-0.26**	-0.31***	-0.28**
11. Meal delivery	-0.24*	—[b]	-0.24*	-0.24*	—[b]	-0.24*
12. Food distribution	-0.18	—[b]	-0.18	-0.35***	—[b]	-0.35***
13. Light housework	0.17	0.02	0.02	0.06	-0.30***	-0.03
14. Heavy housework	-0.27*	-0.07	-0.07	0.01	0.01	0.01
15. Reading/letter writing	—[a]	0.15	0.15	—[a]	-0.35***	-0.35***
16. Employment referral	-0.06	-0.04	-0.04	0.02	-0.41***	-0.41***
17. Emergency assistance	-0.09	-0.17	-0.09	-0.15	-0.17	-0.25**
18. Housing assistance	-0.06	-0.02	-0.02	0.02	-0.42***	-0.42***
19. Information about services	-0.09	-0.22	-0.18	-0.23*	-0.02	-0.11
20. Total number of services	-0.04	-0.07	-0.06	-0.21*	-0.22*	-0.30**

* Significant at the 0.10 level.
** Significant at the 0.05 level.
*** Significant at the 0.01 level.
a No churches offered this service.
b This service was assumed to be formal only.

volved in non-spiritual matters, there was great diversity in this regard among the churches included in this study. Especially in the South, the two dimensions of church conservatism, doctrinal and social, are often confused. The findings presented here corroborate Steinitz's findings that churches with conservative social orientations provided fewer services to older adults.[22] Doctrinal conservatism, in this case, fundamentalism, was not, however, an important predictor of failure to provide most types of services to the elderly.

Linkages between local churches and the social service network in areas similar to Davidson County could possibly facilitate improved service to older adults. The churches in this study offered a wide range of services to their elderly congregants, including many to meet their non-spiritual needs. The data, however, suggest that churches need access to trained personnel and special resources in order to offer certain types of services. These could be provided through partnership with social services agencies. It is not clear, however, if working through churches would be cost efficient or more effective.

Designers of such a collaborative project would have to proceed with care. Churches with liberal social orientations would have to be identified as potential participants. Not all churches would consider such a project appropriate. Another area of concern would be how the introduction of such a program would alter the informal service support systems already functioning in the context of churches. This issue must be carefully explored before formal linkages are considered.

NOTES

1. Paul B. Maves, "Aging, Religion, and the Church," in *Handbook of Social Gerontology*, ed. Clark Tibbits (Chicago: University of Chicago Press, 1960), pp. 698-749.

2. James W. Ellor, S.M. Kanerson-Ray, and Sheldon Tobin, "The Role of the Church in Services for the Elderly," *Interdisciplinary Topics in Gerontology* 17(1983): pp. 119-131.

3. Gordon Streib, "Old Age, Religion, and the Solid South: Observations by a Sociologist," *Southern Gerontologist* 4(1984): 1,5. Sheldon S. Tobin and James W. Ellor, "The Church and the Aging Network: More Interaction Needed," *Generations* Fall (1983): pp. 26-28.

4. James W. Ailor, "The Church Provides for the Elderly," in *Foundations*

in Practical Gerontology, eds. Rosamond R. Boyd and Charles G. Oakes (Columbia, S.C.: University of South Carolina Press, 1969), pp. 191-206. R. Gray and David Moberg, *The Church and the Older Person* (William E. Erdman Publishing Co., 1962).

5. Thomas C. Cook, *The Religious Sector Explores its Mission in Aging* (National Interfaith Coalition on Aging, Inc., 1976).

6. Tobin and Ellor, "Church and Aging Network," pp. 26-28.

7. James W. Ellor and Robert B. Coates, "Examining the Role of the Church in the Aging Network," *Journal of Religion & Aging* (forthcoming).

8. Lucy Y. Steinitz, "The Local Church as Support for the Elderly," *Journal of Gerontological Social Work* 4(1981): pp. 43-53; idem, "The Church within the Network of Social Services to the Elderly: Case Study of Laketown" (Ph.D. diss., University of Chicago, 1980).

9. Maves, "Aging, Religion and Church," pp. 698-749.

10. Steinitz, "Church within Network," pp. 101-105.

11. Samuel S. Hill, *The South and the North in American Religion* (Athens: The University of Georgia Press, 1980), pp. 140-41.

12. Streib, "Old Age, Religion, and South," p. 1.

13. Maves, "Aging, Religion, and Church," pp. 698-749.

14. Charles Hudson, "The Structure of a Fundamentalist Christian Belief System," in *Religion and the Solid South*, eds. Samuel S. Hill, Edgar T. Thompson, Anne Firor Scott, Charles Hudson, and Edwin S. Gaustad (Nashville: Abingdon Press, 1972), pp. 122-142.

15. Steinitz, "Church within Network," p. 170.

16. Ibid.

17. Steinitz, "Church within Network," pp. 40-82. Tobin and Ellor, "Church and Aging Network," pp. 25-28.

18. Steinitz, "Church within Network," pp. 16-39.

19. Tobin and Ellor, "Church and Aging Network," p. 5.

20. Streib, "Old Age, Religion, and South," p. 5.

21. Hill, *South and North in Religion*, pp. 140-141.

22. Steinitz, "Church within Network," pp. 101-105.

Judaism:
Lifestyles Leading to Physical, Mental, and Social Wellbeing in Old Age

A. Michael Davies

The basic moral position of the Jewish religion toward old age is encapsulated in the Fifth Commandment. Not only are we required to honor parents, but there is a reward—the only Commandment in fact, with a reward—longevity. "Thou shalt rise up before the hoary head and honor the fact of the old man and fear thy God," writes Leviticus.[1] Thus respect for and care of the elderly was early established as a fundamental religious tenet. Neglect of elders was seen as heinous crime, and "a nation of fierce countenance which shall not regard the person of the old"[2] was characterized as barbaric.

Throughout the Bible and Talmud the term "elder" is a synonym for sages and judges, and the image is one of wisdom and leadership. However, the transformation of society, accentuated by the dispersion of the Jews after the destruction of the Temple in the year 70, led to a loss of filial support and emergence of the problem of the poor and destitute elderly. To these applied the general precepts of charity and almsgiving, and over the centuries Jewish communities evolved institutions which substituted for the family in case of need.

Permission to publish this material has been granted by the World Health Organization.

DEFINITIONS OF AGING

"The days of our years are 70 years and if by reason of strength, 80 years" wrote the psalmist.[3] The limit of human longevity was laid down as 120 years in Genesis,[4] and from this derives the traditional blessing, "May you live to 120," although the patriarchs are recorded as having considerably exceeded this span. A long life followed by death at "a good old age"[5] was a blessing and a reward for keeping God's statutes and commandments.[6] The Mishnah, listing the characteristics of each age, cites ". . . at forty for discernment, at fifty for counsel, at sixty for old age, at seventy for grey hair, at eighty for sorrow, at ninety for decrepitude and at one hundred as if dead and passed from the world."[7]

The limitations of chronological reckoning were clearly recognized; Samuel says, "I have grown old and grey" when he was only 52,[8] while King David was "very old" at 70.[9] Later, however, there is a certain amount of confusion in Talmudic writings, "elder" became a title of respect for a learned rabbi, whatever his age.[7]

Characteristics of the Elderly

While "old age brings happiness and honor" according to the sayings of the rabbis[10] they also cite the case of Barzillai, "a very aged man, even fourscore years old," who said to the King, "Can I discern between good and bad? Can thy servant taste what I eat or what I drink? Can I hear any more the voices of singing men and singing women?"[11]

The classical allegorical description of the infirmities of old age, some say the beginnings of gerontology, comes from the book of Ecclesiastes, attributed to Solomon at the end of his life: ". . . the years draw nigh when thou shalt say, I have no pleasure in them."[12] These verses have been the subject of extensive commentaries through the ages by both Christians and Jews.[13] The phrase in Ecclesiastes that "the silver cord will be snapped" was interpreted by R. Levi ben Gershon (1285-1344) as referring to the arteries which cease to pulse in old age and fail to convey the spirit to vital organs. The rabbis followed this lead and viewed the later years of life as unattractive. "The rocks have become three tall, the near have become (too) distant (to visit), two (legs) have become three (with a cane) and the peacemaker of the house has ceased (to function as such).'' And again, the old resemble apes, they cannot reason, and a man must pray that in the later years "his eyes may see, his mouth eat, his legs walk, for in old age all powers fail.'' "To an old person, even a small mound appears as the highest mountain,'' says the Talmud, going on to describe the illnesses of old age in detail. There is diminution of the light of his skin and the light of his eyes, of his enthusiasm, his senses and his abilities, all of which force him into the world-to-come with "trembling, anger and fear.'' "The opinions of the elderly change, the judgement of the elderly is unstable.''[14] The physiological changes of old age are exemplified by the hypothermia of King David who approached his 70th year (in which he died) "and they covered him with clothes but he gat no heat.''[15]

The rabbis, however, were well aware of the limitations of this negative stereotype and emphasised the positive aspects of old age, particularly wisdom. "With the ancient is wisdom and in length of days, understanding.''[16] But in spite of this emphasis and the commandments to honor the elderly, there was a general opinion that with age comes loss of intellectual capacity, and even the opinions of the old were not always preferred to those of the young. The dilemma is illustrated by the following citation, which also gives something of the flavor of the Talmudic discussions. "When R. Abbahu claimed authority in a given dispute due to his age, R. Jeremiah answered, 'Is the matter decided by age? — It is decided by reason.'" Targum Onkelos (the Aramaic translation of the Bible) also reflected this view by translating, "You shall rise before the aged" (Lev 19:32) as, "Arise before those knowledgeable in Torah." The rabbis held that even a young scholar is called "elder" and should be honored, while no honor is due to the ignorant or sinful though old. However, Isi b. Judah differed "You shall rise before the aged," i.e., "all the aged." R. Johanan agreed, even concerning gentile elders, but R. Nahman and Rav did not act in this manner. According to Maimonides, "one must honor the exceedingly old, even if they are not wise, by rising.''[13] The majority opinion of the Talmud can be summed up in the statement, "Old age is a crown of thorns," and as Immanuel the Jew of Rome (1261-1328) wrote much later, "Old age is a natural disease."

MORAL PRECEPTS AND THEIR APPLICATION

Honor and Support

Whatever the differences about the decrements of aging and the capacity of the elderly, there was no doubt as to the honor and support due to them. Obligations to the old derived directly from the Commandments, reinforced many times in Holy Writ. So much was this rooted in tradition and practice that Jeremiah lamented the fall of Jerusalem saying, "The faces of the elders were not honored,"[17] and R. Nahman of Bratslav (1772-1811), over 2300 years later, wrote that "the prosperity of a country is in accordance with the treatment of its aged."

The Sages were quite specific about "honor thy father and thy mother" and defined the duties of the children to include the provision of food, drink, clothing and a roof for their parents. Although the first duty was to parents, the principle was extended to brothers and sisters, then neighbors, then fellow townsmen and then strangers in that order, to the extent that the individual was capable of providing help. Those elders who were poor and alone were to be cared for by charity together with other needy. But the rules of giving charity were also strict, and there was much greater merit in the giving by stealth, while ostentation diminished the credit. Everything possible had to be done to diminish the shame of receiving charity. The benefits had to be administered in a way that maintained the dignity of the elder and that did not force him to beg. Circumstances which forced a man to accept charity were a reflection on the family and its inability to meet its obligations.

Religious Burial

Honor transcended death, and a traditional religious burial was promised to every elder, however poor. A very early activity of the Jewish communities, which developed in Europe in the early Middle Ages, after building of the Synagogue, was to establish a graveyard and a burial society (Hevra Kadisha)—a charitable trust to ensure that the dignity of all would be maintained, in death as in life.

Euthanasia

Another belief, that life is a gift of God and of infinite worth, led to the principle that any fraction of life is equally of infinite value. Whatever other concession Jewish law may make for the mitigation and relief of suffering, which carries a high priority, such relief cannot be purchased at the cost of life itself. It has always been forbidden to do anything which could hasten death, even to move a dying patient if that might shorten life. A person on his deathbed, of any age, is a living person in every respect. From this principle derives an absolute opposition to euthanasia under any conditions. On the other hand, in recent years, some rabbis are inclined to sanction the withdrawal of heroic supports which would prolong a lingering life with no hope of recovery. The rationale for this is that one does not thereby hasten death but rather removes an impediment, the life support apparatus, which delays the departure of the soul.

Work and Retirement

Just as life is a gift, work is a duty, and the elderly have a moral obligation to continue a productive life as long as their health and strength permit. With this, however, goes the earliest concept of retirement by virtue of age. The Levites were obliged to serve in the Temple from the age of 25 to the age of 50.[18] The Talmud interprets Numbers 1:3 as requiring retirement from the army by age 60.[19] In the Sanhedrin, the high court and supreme legislative body during the whole of the Roman period, elders were not allowed to serve. The meaning of "elder" is disputed but usually accepted as those with grey hair according to tradition, age 70 and over. In the Dead Sea Sect, no one over 60 could act as a judge.[20]

The rabbis did not extrapolate the compulsory retirement, of the Levites for example, to all organized work; it was pointed out that this was merely a change of occupation, not full retirement. There was also the requirement that the elder continue to study, to keep the commandments all the days of his life and to make some contribution to society, e.g., by productive work, according to his strength and ability. "Work is of itself a defined value."[7] This is notwithstanding the obligation of his family, and of society, to support the elder for, as R. Joshua Pelek laid down 200 years ago, "Even if he has a source of income, he must be occupied with work."[7] These principles continue to guide new forms of social organization (e.g., the kibbutz), although they may be overridden in the modern welfare state where the law and work contracts provide for retirement and where pension schemes exist. The moral obligation to continue to be useful, however, remains.[20]

Duties of the Elder

In addition to being useful, the elder is expected to continue to take an active role in society, to attend communal prayers and to study the law. He is also expected to continue public activities designed to serve his fellows and, where he can, to give charity. As far as possible, he should maintain his autonomy, and the community will help him to do this, so as to be as little a burden as possible to his family and friends. This need to remain independent has had a profound effect on intergenerational relationships among American Jewry and has led to a lower frequency of the three-generation family under one roof.[21] The giving of charity by elders persisted through the Middle Ages to the present day. On an 11th-century Egyptian charity list, a quarter of the named donors were designated as "elders,"[22] while the emancipation of the Jews and the development of industrial society saw the creation of organized charitable trusts frequently maintained by "senior citizens." The development of the American Jewish Joint Distribution Committee, whose help for the elderly is referred to below, is a case in point.[23]

HEALTH AND DISEASE

Maintenance of Health

Exhortations to live frugally as a way to health, bound up with regulations for personal and community hygiene, form part of biblical and early religious writings. The tradition was summarized by Maimonides (1135-1204) in his "regimen sanitatis" which, although not written specifically for the elderly, provides guidance for adults. It was translated in the Middle Ages to Hebrew and Latin from the "Fi Tadbir al-Sihha" (Guide to Good Health) written in

1198 for the Egyptian Sultan, who suffered from depression and from physical symptoms. Physical health is dependent on psychological wellbeing, writes Maimonides, and there must be a regime of health. This includes care of the body and its functions, physical activity, proper breathing, work, diet, family and sexual life. Music, poetry, paintings and walks in pleasant surroundings all have a part to play in the maintenance of health and of inner peace.

Maimonides was the outstanding rabbinical teacher and philosopher of the Middle Ages and has had enormous influence on subsequent Jewish religious thought.[24] His teachings and aphorisms are still accepted as a guide to religious and secular practice among observant Jews, and his attitudes to positive health have become part of the tradition.

Duties of the Sick Elder

The sick at all ages are enjoined to seek expert advice and to regulate their lives according to the instructions of their medical attendants. Their duty is to get well; the saving of life, in the Jewish tradition, puts aside all other commandments. Thus the elder may eat on fast days or break the Sabbath if his health requires it, and similar transgressions are permitted to his doctors if health will thereby be improved or suffering abated. That is not to say that commandments should not be kept in so far as the patient is able and to the degree that observance does not damage his health. In other words, his life style should be altered only when his health requires it, although the interpretation of that phrase is very liberal.

The principle of preservation of life style and self esteem of the sick elderly has led certain religious groups in Israel to build old age homes for their members where customs can be maintained while integrating modern geriatric nursing and physiotherapy services into their regime.

The Evolution of Social Institutions

No attempt was made in Talmudic times to create special institutions to help the aged nor were there specific regulations for their care. If not living among the family, as was customary, destitute aged people were treated as part of the general social problems of weakness and poverty and cared for through the general precepts of charity. "The transitions from the position of powerful elder to that of an aged pauper requiring special assistance outside the frame of the family is an outcome of the heritage of Judaic-Muslim-Christian civilization."[25]

The Synagogue

The synagogue was always the focus of instruction and social activity as well as religious activity in the small, dispersed Jewish communities that developed in the Diaspora after the year 70. The aged were singled out in medieval times as worthy objects of charity administered from the synagogue. There was also an early tradition of visiting the sick and bringing food and clothing. This was often organized in later centuries by the wife of the rabbi of the congregation with the help of other worthy women.

The fact that the synagogue was used as the center of continued study meant that many elders would stay on after morning prayers to fulfill the commandment of learning the law. There was the secondary function of providing shelter and companionship and to this day, in many of the more religiously observant Jewish communities, the synagogue is the old man's club.

Under ghetto conditions, toward the Middle Ages and subsequently, the function of the synagogue as a communal center assumed increasing importance. Social needs of the present day, particularly in the United States, have tended to turn the synagogue into an all-embracing social center, including, where appropriate, a service club for the elderly and a focus for home care.

From Hekdesh to Hospital and Old Age Home

The rabbis of the Talmud were very much aware of the changes in the role of the elder within the family, even in those days, and supported the creation of homes for the elderly "to withhold worry and sorrow from the elder and from his family and environment."[10]

The "Bet hekdesh l'aniyim" (house consecrated to the needy), hekdesh for short, probably existed in the early Jewish communities and seems to have been adopted by the early Christian church and evolved into the medieval hospital. The early hekdesh was a religiously motivated charitable trust that did not differentiate between the traveler, the poor and the sick. The Emperor Julian called on the Romans to establish houses for the poor wayfarer and the sick "like the Jews among whom there are no beggars."[26] A document from Cologne in the 11th century describes the existence of such a hostel, and by the 14th century such "hospitals" were recorded in Barcelona, Munich and Regensberg. Contemporary documents in the 13th to 15th centuries suggest that only strangers and the very poor were housed there, however, and gradually the hekdesh degenerated into an asylum for the poorest of the poor, particularly the poor elderly, the form in which it persisted in the ghettos of Russia and Poland up to this century.

With the population growth of Christian Europe during the Middle Ages, the term, "hospital" was used more and more for institutions dealing with sick people. Jewish hospitals, in the modern sense, are recorded from 1740 onwards in Europe and coexisted, apparently, with the hekdesh.[27] There were signs of differentiation before this date, however, and a hospice specifically for the needy and afflicted poor was established by Mordecai Meisel in Prague in the 1580s.[28]

By the second half of the 18th century, the break-up of the traditional family cohesion in the richer and more emancipated Jewish communities of Western Europe had begun, while old age began to be perceived as a social problem separate from poverty. There was also the developing gap between the older, more conservative generation and the younger, more emancipated one, with the growing need to find solutions for the poor and estranged elderly. Thus, homes for the elderly were founded, in Amsterdam in 1749,[25] in Berlin in 1829, in Hamburg ten years later, and so on. By the end of the 19th century, most large Jewish communities of Europe had a home for the elderly together with a charitable trust for the support of the aged in their own homes.

The poorer communities of Eastern Europe and the more tradition-oriented Jewish communities in Arab lands have followed this same path of evolution of services but more slowly, so that the hekdesh or its equivalent was still found at the beginning of this century.

BACK TO COMMUNITY SERVICES

Where living standards permitted and where social mobility was great, particularly in the United States and Canada, the application of the basic religious principles referred to above took the form of new approaches to the provision of comprehensive care for the elderly by the community. Starting with homes for the poor and sick elderly, several of the larger Jewish communities pioneered the development of a spectrum of institutions ranging from sheltered and special purpose housing through residential and skilled nursing units. The more advanced communities linked these with a network of community services, including golden age clubs, meals on wheels, and welfare and nursing services for those who could stay in their own homes and wished to do so. Over the years, these multifarious services came to be managed by professional social workers but with funding from the community and with a strong backing of volunteer workers.[25]

By the time we reach the modern period, it is clear that the design and provision of services becomes that of the society of each country. While signs of Jewish tradition may still be visible, the differences between services to the different communities have become increasingly blurred over recent decades as all have come to accept the same universal religious and humanistic values.

Recent Developments

There are several examples from recent years which indicate the high priority still given to the status and wellbeing of the elderly and the continuing application of moral principles to new situations. Part of the continued Jewish awareness derives from the high proportion of elderly among Jews and the consequence of the Holocaust, and partly because of the new challenges in Israel and elsewhere.

DEMOGRAPHY OF THE JEWS

A high proportion of elderly has long been a characteristic of Jewish communities. Already in the last century, the proportion of infants in the Jewish populations of Europe was lower than that of their non-Jewish neighbors, while the proportion of the elderly was higher. In 1975, 14.2% of world Jewry was aged 65 and over, and the prediction for the year 2000 is 16.4%,[29] a figure to be achieved by most developed nations only in 2025. By the end of this century, the percentage of Jews aged 75 and over will rise to 7.3%, a proportion higher than that of some Scandinavian countries. This experience has, perhaps, added urgency to the search for solutions to the burden of aging, particularly in European and Israeli communities.

An extreme example of one new challenge is that of some Eastern European communities where, due to the ravages of the Holocaust, conversion and migration of the young, the average age is very high and the community is, literally, dying out. In some of these, particularly in Rumania, an attempt has been made, with the help of the "Joint" (see below) to redesign the institutions of the community. Not only is there a great increase in the supply of social services and accommodation in the old age homes and long term care facilities, but the cultural life has been reorganized, the theatre for example, to facilitate the active participation of the elderly, so that the last years may be spent usefully and with dignity.

A high proportion of the immigrants to Israel after 1948 were survivors of Hitler's Europe and thus older, while subsequent immigration from a number of countries (Morocco, Poland, Russia and the United States, for example) has favored the elderly. Thus, the proportion of those over 65 has increased rapidly, within the Jewish population from 3.7% in 1950 to 9.7% in 1980, and will reach over 10% by 1990.[30] Although these proportions are not impressive by European standards, the *rate* of increase has given rise to some concern and a search for innovative solutions.

THE "JOINT"

The American Jewish Joint Distribution Committee was established in 1914 as an organization for the "rescue, relief and reconstruction" of Jewish society wherever in the world that help might be needed, having the motto "my brother's keeper."[23] Their first activity was to send support to the besieged Jewish community of Jerusalem, caught in famine between the Turkish and British forces. In his report of how the money was spent, Hoofien wrote in 1918,

> . . . when we could begin to form further classification of the destitute, we first of all devoted our attention to the old, aged men and women, who were without support from their children. Till then, I had, in all cases . . . had them enter into one of the Old Aged Homes . . . But there was a limit to the capacity of these homes and it was also much to be questioned if it was desirable to continue to increase the number of inmates . . . So a regular weekly support . . . was arranged for. . . . [31]

In 1949, an agreement was concluded between the "Joint" and the Israeli Ministry of Health to establish "Malben" (Institutions for the Care of Handicapped Immigrants) for the joint care of the aged, infirm and handicapped who were flooding into Israel. Particular attention was given to the elderly, many of whom were survivors of the Holocaust and without living relatives. Once emergency needs were under control, Malben began to consolidate its own direct care services as well as to promote the development of municipal and community facilities for the elderly. These measures included cash relief, constructive loans to enable them to earn a living, home welfare and health services and the establishment of community based "golden age" clubs. An important principal was the need to maintain personal dignity. One way to do this was through the development of sheltered workshops where the elderly could work at their own pace. It has proved possible to transform the functions of the institutions as needs and pressures have changed and to discharge many to care in the community. [32] Thus the activities illustrate the provision of the traditional emergency care with facilitation of ways to maintain autonomy of elders in the community according to modern Western concepts.

Outside Israel, the "Joint" has programs in aging in each of the 30 countries in which it operates. It is estimated that half of its 1984 budget of $46.5 million will benefit the aged of the Jewish world. [33]

THE KIBBUTZ

The early kibbutzim were usually founded as cooperative agricultural settlements by groups of young adults. These founding fathers and mothers are now grandparents and great-grandparents, and the way the kibbutz has dealt with the problems of aging is an interesting fusion of Jewish tradition and pragmatic socialism. The raison d'etre was work, work of the individual for the benefit of the commune, with the commune providing all of his or her needs. As the years passed and the founders grew older, the number of daily hours of work required was reduced according to age, but never to zero, and work is expected, as in Talmudic days, of all who are well enough to participate. While the lighter jobs have always been given to the weaker, there is a limit to such possibilities in agriculture, so many kibbutzim have introduced light industry as a supplementary source of income. In later years the type of industry has been selected by some with an eye to the ability and special conditions needed by the elderly worker, even though this has often meant a change in the economic basis of the cooperative.

The kibbutz pays special attention to the parents of its members, and its members when older, by providing choice accommodation, and a slightly higher standard of living while ensuring continued full participation in the cultural and social life of the group. In some, the admission of parents or elderly retired relatives has required a non-religious kibbutz to build a synagogue and provide kosher food to meet their needs. Thus, the traditional moral principles are still observed and the spirit of "honor thy father and thy mother" has been adapted to a new way of life.

NOTES

1. Leviticus 19:32.
2. Deuteronomy 28:50.
3. Psalms 90:10.
4. Genesis 6:3.
5. Genesis 15:15.
6. Deuteronomy 6:2.

7. M. Kurtz. Attitudes to aging in Jewish tradition. In: Bergman, S. and Margolec, Y. (Eds.) Aging and Aged in Israel Tel Aviv, Am Oved Publishers, 1984, pp. 11-40 (Hebrew).

8. I Samuel 12:2.

9. I Kings 1:15.

10. Sh. Y. Cohen. The concept of old age in Jewish thought. Assia (Jerusalem 9(4):13-24, 1983 (Hebrew).

11. 2 Samuel 19:32-35.

12. Ecclesiastes 12:2-7.

13. Hebrew Encyclopedia. "Aging in Jewish sources," 16:966-970; Jerusalem, 1963 (Hebrew).

14. Talmud Shabbat, 152 a.b.

15. 1 Kings 1:1.

16. Job 11:12.

17. Lamentations 5:12.

18. Leviticus 8:23-26.

19. Talmud Baba Bitra, 121b.

20. M. Slae. 1 Mandatory retirement as a function of age — Jewish sources. Assia (Jerusalem) 9(4):49-55, 1983 (Hebrew).

21. J. Yaffe. The American Jews. New York, Random House, 1968, pp. 285-286.

22. N. A. Stillman. The Jews of Arab Lands. Philadelphia, Jewish Publication Society, 1979, p. 196.

23. O. Handlin. A Continuing Task: The American Jewish Joint Distribution Committee. 1914-1964 New York, Random House, 1964.

24. Encyclopedia Judaica. "Maimonides, Moses," 11:754-751, Jerusalem, 1971.

25. Encyclopedia Judaica. "Age and the aged." 2:344-348, Jerusalem, 1972.

26. H. Friedenwald. Notes on the history of Jewish hospitals, in "The Jews and Medicine," Baltimore, Johns Hopkins Press, Vol. II, 1944, pp. 514-518.

27. Encyclopedia Judaica. "Hospitals," 8:1034-1039, Jerusalem, 1972.

28. J.R. Marcus. The Jew in the Medieval World. New York, Atheneum, 1978, p. 324.

29. U.O. Schmelz. "Aging of World Jewry." Jerusalem, Hebrew University Institute of Contemporary Jewry and Brookdale Institute of Gerontology and Adult Human Development, 1984. (Jewish Population Studies No. 15.)

30. A.M. Davies. "Epidemiology and services for the elderly," in "Colloque: Epidemiologie et medicine communantaire." Paris, INSERM, 1984, pp. 217-229.

31. Report of Mr. S. Hoofien to the Joint Distribution Committee of the American Friends for Jewish War Sufferers. New York, November 1918, p. 89.

32. J. Margulec. Personal communication.

33. J. Habib, in "Preface" to Reference 29.

The Teachings of Confucianism on Health and Old Age

Takehiko Okada

The *Book of History*, one of the classics of Confucianism, refers in its Hung Fan (The Great Plan) to the Five Blessings of Life: Long Life, Riches, Health of Body and Peace of Mind, Love of Virtue, and Natural and Timely Death. Now Virtue here comprises, of course, such virtues as are based on ethics and upheld by Confucianism. The very fact that love of virtue is counted among human blessings shows that Confucianism underlies this view of happiness.

Why is long life mentioned first of all the Five Blessings? It is because Confucianists believe that one can enjoy happiness chiefly through the gift of long life. Later Confucianists say that long life enables people to enjoy life fully, gives knowledge as well as ability to make what has been impossible possible, and advances understanding and learning. In a word, it is necessary for achievement of the ideals of Confucianism that people should keep healthy and enjoy long life. It goes without saying that a frivolous life with scarcely any aspiration to seek the meaning of life is against the teachings of Confucianism, however long the lifespan may be.

In Hung Fan, Lu Chi (Six Evils) are also mentioned: Premature Death (through disasters), Sickness, Anxiety, Poverty, Stubbornness (resulting in disasters), and Weak Will (resulting in humiliation). We should bear in mind further that, according to the *Book of History*, the Five Blessings are obtained only when one is obedient to the will of the Supreme. When one is against it, evils are sure to result. In I Hsun (The Instruction of I Yin) it is stated: "Providence

Permission to publish this material has been granted by the World Health Organization.

is not inflexible. The Supreme sends down manifold blessings to the good, and manifold disasters to the evil.''

The *Book of History* also states that human happiness depends on obedience to the absolute moral authority of the Supreme. This philosophy of happiness is naturally based on a moralistic views of life, of society, and of the world in general. In Confucianism all teachings about health, for the old as well as for the young, are argued from this viewpoint.

In Chinese thought there are various teachings about keeping healthy. They are different in accordance with differences in the views of life, of society, and of the world. Roughly speaking, we can distinguish three main currents in the history of ideas in China. First, there is idealism based on the moral nature of humanity. Confucianism belongs to this group. Second, there is realism based on the moral nature of humanity. Legalism, strategism, and Machiavellianism belong here. Third, there is transcendentalism based on the religious nature of humanity. Taoism and Buddhism belong to this third group.

With its emphasis on morality, Confucianism is based on a universalism which regards Self and Other as one. From this viewpoint, to lead a good life and to help others lead a good life are related to each other. According to this idea, cultivation of character and development of one's country are considered as two sides of one ideal, though the former is acknowledged as the more fundamental. Cultivation of character, with its emphasis on human relations, is achieved through good government, and good government, in its turn, is brought about through cultivation of good character. In this sense, cultivation of character can be called the foundation of good government. Thus, all in all, it is of the utmost importance to keep heaven-given life sound and healthy. We see it as natural that many teachings on health should be found in Confucianism.

Those who are guided by realism take a utilitarian view of life. They view Self and Other in a relationship of opposition and strife, wherein both parties seek means to control the other. Naturally, they are indifferent to both ethics and religion, and few, if any, teachings on health are found among their sayings.

Taoism and Buddhism, on the other hand, based on the religious side of humanity, are somewhat fatalistic in that they regard human life as inevitably beset with worries because of lusts. They seek salvation in believing in the Supreme, thereby achieving eternal life. Their teachings on health are promulgated from this viewpoint.

Thus, in China, Confucianism, Taoism, and Buddhism included teachings on health and keeping long life. In China, as well as in other countries, teachings on health were given with a view not only to the physical, but also to the spiritual and social wellbeing of the people. In Taoism more than in Confucianism this standpoint was emphasized and characteristically developed.

Taoism at first laid emphasis on the social and the spiritual sides of humanity. Not only seeking ways to keep healthy, it sought to get rid of lusts by subtle maneuvering of the mind, thereby trying to achieve an eternal life which is free from lusts and enlightened in the truest sense of the word. In later generations, however, there was a tendency to seek such freedom in the body, and as a result, surprisingly various teachings about health were given.

It may not be too much to say that the fundamental difference in the teachings of Confucianism and of Taoism on health lies in their respective relations to ethics. Every teaching of Confucianism is firmly founded on ethics, as we have seen in the example of the *Book of History*.

It is well known that benevolence is regarded by Confucianists as the highest virtue of all the virtues and as containing all the virtues. Confucius himself attached importance to benevolence, saying, "The benevolent are long-lived," meaning that benevolence is the way to long life. He said, too, "Filial Piety and Fraternal Love — are they not the root of virtue, especially the former?" The following statement, which we find in the Canon of Filial Piety, elucidates Confucius' point: "Our hair and our skin, namely everything pertaining to our bodies, we inherit from our parents. It is the beginning of filial piety not to injure them. To be virtuous and make our family name known to the world is the end of filial piety." According to Confucianism, then, our bodies are the valuable legacy of our parents. To keep our bodies uninjured is, therefore, regarded as the root of filial piety. Its final object, however, is cultivation of character, and our parents are honored when our good names are known to the world.

Because Confucianism essentially values ethics and attaches importance to morality, there may seem to be conflict between the demands of virtue and the demands of filial piety. "The earnest scholar and the man of virtue will not seek to live at the expense of their virtues. They will sacrifice their lives willingly in order to preserve their virtues complete." It is maintained that one will sometimes find it necessary to sacrifice one's own life to fulfill the demands of justice. Yet, is not this statement contradictory to the idea that keeping our bodies uninjured is the root of filial piety?

Confucianists considered that in fulfilling the demands of justice in society, there are emergency laws as well as peacetime laws, neither of which are contrary to justice. To sacrifice one's own life for justice is in accordance with emergency laws, and it is not contradictory to the command to keep one's life uninjured.

It was Ekiken Kaibara, a famous Japanese Confucianist of the Tokugawa Era, who emphasized from this viewpoint the importance of keeping healthy. He maintained that every human event has two sides. In peacetime one should try to preserve one's life to the best of one's ability. Yet, it sometimes happens that one should sacrifice one's own life in an emergency, and one must adapt oneself to the occasion. Only those people who try their best to keep healthy in peacetime will be able to meet the demands of an emergency and show courage.

Later Confucianists argued human existence from a more profound philosophical standpoint. This tendency was a result of the influence of Taoism and Buddhism. According to them, everything in the Universe is generated by *li* (reason) and *chi* (force). *Chi* is the material; *li* is the root of existence and the norm. *Li* in a thing is *Hsing* (nature). Man is composed of the purest of *chi*. In *Hsing* man finds ethics and moral will. Those later Confucianists considered *li* and *chi* mutually in the relationship of brotherhood and everything in the Universe as their partners.

In its generation theory, Confucianism is far from mechanical materialism. Its world view is that humanity has an ultimate purpose in life. It is firmly based on ethics, considering every object in the Universe as having a proper purpose to be accomplished. Thus, "to generate" is considered the greatest virtue.

The Confucian idea of filial piety gained depth by the influence of the generation theory, which helped people to feel gratitude not only for their elders but also for everything in Nature as forces which nurture them. Gratitude was felt for producers of food, for teachers, for rulers, and finally for the Power behind the Universe. To feel gratitude, and to try to do one's best as an expression of the feeling of gratitude, is an attitude resulting from this idea. There is even something religious in such an attitude. *Yojokun* (The Motto for Health), by Ekiken Kaibara, expostulates the standpoint that

> one should be dutiful to one's parents and to the Universe, and endeavor to behave virtuously, mindful of one's relations to others, to enjoy long life and be happy. This is what every man desires. For that purpose, one should learn from the teachings of one's ancestors, and master ways to keep healthy. This is the foremost importance in life. One's body is immeasurably valuable. Nothing can replace it. It is utterly foolish not to know proper ways to keep healthy, to get addicted to lusts, and, as a result of the corruption, to lose one's life.

It is natural that Ekiken, as a Confucianist, should criticize the arguments on health of what he called "vulgar people," the sham Confucianists and Taoists:

> Vulgar people are apt to get addicted to lusts and be ungrateful to Nature. They don't nurture *chi* and for that reason are unable to enjoy long life. Taoists, though they attach importance to nurture of *chi*, disregard reason. Sham Confucianists lay too much stress on reason, and neglect *chi*. They don't know how to cultivate character, so they fail to keep long life. They are both far from the ways of men of high virtue.

Ekiken was an erudite scholar who had a good knowledge of Neo-Confucianism, which was influential in the Era of Sung-Ming in China. He exerted great influence in the fields of practical science and botany, and his teachings on the ways of keeping healthy were versatile and detailed. In his teachings, the importance of quiet sitting, seated meditation as in Buddhism, abdominal breathing and Taoist breathing were stressed. We must, however, recall here that he was not the only Confucianist who attached importance to this practical side of Confucianism.

What is remarkable is that Ekiken dedicated several pages in his *Yojokun* to the care of the old, telling the young what they should bear in mind. The young people should do their utmost to make it possible for the old to enjoy life. They should satisfy their needs as much as possible, and try not to anger or worry them. The young should also keep the bedrooms and the sitting rooms of old people clean and in order, and cook nutritious and delicious meals for them. Old people often have stomach troubles, so in preparing their dishes utmost care should be taken.

The old themselves are advised to enjoy life, nurture *chi*, and take care not to fall ill. Enjoyment of life is the foundation of Ekiken's teachings on health. A day is much more precious for the old than for the young. For the old, time flies more quickly. They value a day ten times as much as the young. Ekiken said: "The old should be reluctant to waste time. They should live on day as ten days, ten days as a hundred days, one month as one year. They should enjoy every minute of their life. Tranquil living without being troubled by lusts is ideal. They should try their best to keep their own bodies healthy." Enjoyment of life, as Ekiken understood it, is different from the idea of vulgar people, who regard satisfaction of desires as the first condition of happiness. He was of the opinion that enjoyment of life should be based on the natural disposition of people, which contains both reason and ethics. There are two kinds of pleasure — negative and positive, what concerns oneself and what concerns things. They are related to each other and are difficult to differentiate. The following is the outline of what Ekiken says in the *Yojokun*.

1. Old people often grumble. They are easy to get angry, oftener than in their young days. When something is against their will, they blame their young. If they do not amend their ways, they will not be able to end their life contentedly. The old should restrain their lusts, control their temper, and be patient. They should not blame their children even when they neglect their filial duties. Thus they may enjoy every minute of their life.
2. They should be tolerant towards their children. Even when people are impolite and impertinent, it is better to accept

wrongs calmly as the way of the world. They should spend their days contentedly without fretting, trusting in Providence.

3. Don't think too much of past mistakes. It is useless to mope away your days. Rid your heart of worries. Enjoy life whenever you can.
4. Spend quiet hours in your room every morning. Recite the Confucian Canon and remove worries from your heart.
5. Dust your desk and seat clean. Always keep your inkstone case in order.
6. Enjoy heaven and earth, mountains and rivers, sceneries, seasons, trees and flowers.
7. Take a walk sometimes in your garden. Appreciate Nature's beauty. To stand in high places will help you to keep your heart free and clear of worries.
8. Nurture *chi* and try not to injure it. Old people are apt to be too careful. Keep your spirits up.
9. Breathe in and out calmly.
10. Don't speak too much or too hastily. Don't speak, laugh, and sing loudly.
11. Don't walk too much. Avoid carrying heavy loads. Don't waste your spirits in unnecessary worries.
12. Don't take part in other people's affairs when you are not needed (funerals and mournings). Don't get too friendly with vulgar people.
13. Sit in a comfortable posture. Lean against a backrest and don't lie down when you can help it.
14. Take good care of yourself, lest you should fall ill.
15. Don't work too much. Remember that old people are easily tired.
16. Don't overeat. Eat small amounts of good, nutritious food. In summer, when the weather is hot and humid, take rests and keep your stomach in good condition.

Catholicism, Lifestyles, and the Wellbeing of the Elderly

Carmen Barros

How has Catholicism resulted in a peculiar lifestyle, and how does this lifestyle limit or enhance the possibilities of the elderly to experience different kinds of wellbeing?

First of all, it seems necessary to begin by clarifying the meaning of the three terms, *Lifestyle*, *Catholicism*, and *Wellbeing*, and to try to relate them in conceptual terms. Then, the second part will deal with the specific content of the Catholic's lifestyle in relation to physical, mental and social wellbeing.

CLARIFICATION OF THE CONCEPTS

Lifestyles is an ambiguous notion. There are several conceptions involved in it. One, connected with the ecological school, is the idea of "genre de vie," or patterns of living, in the sense of concrete expressions of a society's ongoing way of dealing with nature: sets of techniques cemented through traditions whereby human groups secured the material necessities of life. The anthropological view conceptualized it as more or less synonymous with "civilization," that is, the prevailing modes of production and mental structures dominant in a society. It is an integration of modes of behavior and manners of expression. Another notion is given by the psychologist Alfred Adler who conceived it as a schema of drives, feeling, thinking, and perceptions. It conforms to an individually unique

---

Permission to publish this material has been granted by the World Health Organization.

way of living and goal-striving. It is something like a "mode-of-being in the world." This last meaning is the one which seems more pertinent in relation to Catholicism.[1]

Catholicism[2] will be analyzed from a sociological point of view, that is: as a world view, as a well-rounded definition of reality which entails a set of final values that constitute the fundamental objectives that must guide human behavior and social life; as an interpretation about God, human nature, and the types of relationships among men and between men and God; and as a formal organization, that is, the Catholic Church. Catholicism as a world may be characterized in a highly selective and simplistic way.[3] Firstly, it proposes a supra-mundane God, the Creator. Secondly, it is a religion of salvation; in other words, it holds out the promise of deliverance from suffering to its adherents, gives compensatory promises of a better life in the hereafter, explains suffering and dying, and proposes other-wordly solution. Thirdly, the path to salvation is working in this world in accordance with God's commandments. Man has to implement God-willed actions. Fourthly, the highest conception of salvation is redemption, that is, liberation from distress, sickness, suffering and death; salvation from barriers to the infinite which express themselves in suffering, misery and death; salvation for eternal bliss in a paradisiacal future existence. In other words, redemption has to do with the overcoming of something in the actual world which is experienced as senseless.

It should be mentioned that Catholicism has been a highly spiritual religion. Consequently, its influence is exerted mainly through the internalization by the individual believer of its values, beliefs and meanings, which results in a peculiar mode-of-being in the world, especially in terms of a shared schema of motivations, perceptions, feelings and evaluations.

A word of warning: these days, when speaking about Catholicism, one refers to a religious conception that even for many Catholics is only part of a more global, and a very complex, world view. Moreover, Catholics live in a world marked by a process of desacralization, where religious beliefs have lost part of their force. As a result, now Catholics tend to be mild believers. Furthermore, the main features of social organizations are inspired by the values of industrialization and its rationalistic creed which emphasized topics such as ever-increasing production, economic success, efficacy, and efficiency.

Wellbeing is fundamentally a subjective assessment about a factual state. It has to do with the degree of satisfaction of men's needs and aspirations, in this case of those of the elderly. According to the specific types of needs that are being satisfied, it is possible to differentiate between physical, mental and social wellbeing. Nevertheless, this is mainly an analytical distinction because when an individual experiences dissatisfaction in one aspect of his life, it is difficult to experience wellbeing at all.

The purpose of this monograph is to analyze the conceptual elements of Catholicism[1] that result in peculiar traits of a lifestyle that limits or enhances the possibilities of the elderly[2] in order to satisfy their needs and aspirations. Although one of the main characteristics of Catholicism is its universalism, we will deal in part with the universal principles and in part with the peculiarities that it assumes in practice in Latin America. Speaking about "the elderly" entails a high level of abstraction that allows us to disregard all the variations typical in real life. In this case the omissions are very important, such as differences due to social class, family status, and age specific groups.

In order to accomplish this purpose it is necessary to examine which are the needs that, when satisfied, result in a state of physical, mental and social wellbeing, and which are the elements of Catholicism that may influence these achievements either positively or negatively.

ASPECTS OF THE CATHOLIC LIFESTYLE RELATED TO SPECIFIC DIMENSIONS OF WELLBEING

Physical Wellbeing

Physical wellbeing depends on the degree of satisfaction of material needs such as food, health, housing, etc.

In contemporary societies, in general, opportunities to achieve this state of need satisfaction depend on the availability of an adequate income in order to buy necessary goods and services. Other influential factors are the degree of functional capacity and the state of health of the individual. As a matter of fact, the aging process actually goes along with a tendency toward a decrease in income because retirement pensions are in general smaller than wages. At the same time, the probabilities of getting ill increase, and dexterity, strength, energy levels and power of the senses decrease.

Thus, the elderly face two main problems that constrain their possibilities to experience a state of wellbeing. These are the precariousness of their income and the decrease in their functional capabilities, which combine to make all aspects of life more difficult and may even result in dependency on others.

Catholicism is concerned with income only in cases of poverty. Neither does it provide norms that could help to prevent the loss of functional capacities, such as patterns of intake of food, habits of consumption of alcohol and tobacco, etc. In relation to such practices, Catholicism defines extreme behavior as vicious and recommends temperance. It says nothing about physical activity and very little about corporal care. In sum, one may say that Catholicism does not directly enhance the practice of more healthy ways of living. Strictly speaking, in Catholicism there is nothing to induce a specific motivation for the individual to strive for material goods or for developing one's body. So, in a very simplistic way, one may say that even though Catholicism has very little to say about physical wellbeing, it has a great indirect effect on it through psychological factors.

In contrast, it plays a crucial role in taking care of people in need. Catholicism, by conceiving of everybody as brothers, and by defining charity as the main value, has a strong influence on the family, the Church and all the Catholic believers feeling responsible for the elderly in need.

A valid index of this attitude of responsibility is the great number of very ancient beneficial organizations in charge of providing assistance to the elderly poor and the several religious congregations created for this purpose. Charity is the base for social solidarity and is the incentive for collective action in favor of the welfare of the needy.

There is also a second source of support that is very remarkable. Attending to the care of old parents is a must of the Fourth Commandment. There is an emphasis on the family as the object of apostolic commitment. This induces the call for support of the elderly through buttressing the family's role of care and emotional support.

It seems pertinent to comment on two aspects of this attitude of charity, which is one of the peculiar traits of the Catholic style of life. First of all, charity implies commiseration, compassion, love for the other, and the moral obligation of giving to the needy. Therefore, it emphasizes more the duty of the one who gives help and less the rights of the one who receives it. Consequently, there is a risk of helping the elderly in order to satisfy not their needs as defined by themselves but needs defined by the ones in charge, and to meet these needs in the same way for all individuals, disregarding their particularities.

Thus, there is often a sort of assistance where the elderly person is an "object" of charity and the help is defined from above and in equal terms for all the elderly, irrespective of their individual differences. However, also very often the opposite way of behavior happens, that is, respect of the elderly because he is the image of God. Both tendencies coexist.

There has also been a tendency to define daily living as a private issue, leading to the proposition of measures to be implemented mainly through private initiative and volunteer efforts, disregarding the level of public policies. These days in Latin America, however, this tendency is changing. The emphasis now is the commitment to the poor. This new emphasis has reduced the importance of the traditional target of charity — the elderly and the orphans — in favor of a new approach that helps all the needy to organize themselves in order to help themselves. One example of this new type of organization is the Old Age Clubs.

Mental Wellbeing

Mental wellbeing is related to the satisfaction of multiple needs, such as the need to love and be loved, the need to accomplish, the need to feel life as something that is worthwhile and meaningful to be lived. This monograph will deal only with the last issue, because it seems the one over which Catholicism has a very crucial influence.

If one remembers the content of the previous chapter it is obvious that life could appear too hard for the elderly, because it may entail too much pain, too many losses and disappointments.[1] In view of this situation, the questions are: Why is all this bearable? How do you find meaning to pain, decay, greed and sorrow?

Catholicism makes it bearable through some representations and ideas that give a general definition of man and his environment. This notion of identity is particularly necessary in situations of threat, uncertainty and breakdown, because it provides a set of instructions as to how the situations are maintained or repaired. These ideas are internalized in the mind of the believers so as to inhibit anxiety and fear, and to shape and control personal motivation. This is done through three specific forms of attributions or meaning which are of special importance: the one given to life in general, those of suffering and death, and the one related to one's own existence.

Meaning of Life

Catholicism values life because it is a gift of God, the Creator, irrespective of its specific content in each particular individual. It is a gift given to man in order that during it he can reach, if he adapts his behavior to God's commandments, his ultimate goal of the eternal life in paradise. In that sense life is seen as a path with different stages and obstacles that man has to walk because it leads to the true destiny, that is, the bliss of eternal life. In other words, the conception about human life has nothing to do with decay or decline; instead it means an ever-increasing spiritual development and life lasting opportunities of achievement. The goal of human life is not to have more but to be better in terms of spiritual perfection, which is a lifelong task.[1]

Therefore this conception is a safeguard against what Gide said, "the spirit falls into boredom when it has no goals left. . . ." Catholicism can bring the individual above meeting only the basic need, to look for universal values and to perceive a transcendental meaning to life.

Meaning of Suffering and Death

One of the main functions of Catholicism is to give answers to the problem of the meaning of illness, suffering and death, which are inescapable in human life, but insoluble in purely human and scientific terms. Catholicism does this by the attribution of a different meaning to the existential difficulties. It rationalizes sorrow and frustrations. As Jesus suffered in order to redeem us, our own suffering will redeem us from our sins and thus will allow us to obtain salvation and the eternal bliss. In other words, pain is much more acceptable when it is seen as a test that one has to approve in order to obtain the supreme prize of heaven, than when it is perceived as only the sign of decay and the ending of one's self.

Furthermore, Catholicism is a source of comfort, solace or assurance in the face of external stresses and frustrations. It offers the figure of a protective father, and therefore the individual's response has to be one of submission, in imitation of Jesus, the dutiful Son.

In brief, Catholicism: (1) gives arguments in pro of a vicarious sense of security and control over one's life; (2) provides the basis for an attitude of confidence, and for a perception that one is coping with difficulties; (3) allows a deferred or fantasied satisfaction in relation to keenly experienced frustrations and sorrows.

THE MEANING OF ONE'S OWN LIFE

Old age used to be the moment for questioning the purpose of life, and assessing the meaning of one's own life. It is the moment for wondering whether one has really been successful as a human being.

Kierkegaard says we come into the world with sealed papers. In old age, presumably most of the mystery has been revealed; the data is in, though its meaning may be unclear or absent. Maybe the real vocation of old age is to assess its meaning. The answer is very important, because as Erik Erikson said, "the final stage of life is spent in either integrity or despair." There are those who are full of regret and sorrow, and those who integrate their life's meaning and reach understanding. The ideal old person is someone with a sense of control, someone who is able to take charge, someone who has come to terms with life.

At this moment, the self might undertake perhaps the fundamental task at this time, a search for the meaning of its past history. This process of review through reminiscing could result either in a bitter regret that one's life cannot be relived and not enough time remains to start over. In this context, despair and a sense of the end of things can easily set in. Or it could result in a feeling that one has been able to come to terms with life, to reinterpret the past in terms that allows new healings and so adds to the sense of wholeness. In this process the Catholic faith is very helpful. Particularly relevant are the themes not only of repentance for the errors, even more so the assurance of forgiveness and therefore the possibility of reconciliation with God and with oneself, and the faith in redemption and eternal life.

In brief, Catholic doctrine helps to salvage one's dignity as a human being in spite of any kind of miseries that could have happened, to make sense out of what appears as senseless and to bring the life cycle to a fine completion.

Social Wellbeing

Social wellbeing is related to the degree of satisfaction of mainly two closely related types of needs: the need to feel worthwhile and deserving respect from society, and the need to feel a useful and integrated member of society.

The Need to Feel Worthwhile and Respected

Catholicism argues that human beings are to be valued because they are created in the image of God, irrespective of the particular characteristics of each individual. This notion is the essence of human dignity, and constitutes the prime basis for respecting human beings, and for the demand for social equality. This is, of course, the other side of the individual's possibilities of feeling that he is being respected and valued by the other human beings.

The notion that all men are God's children is the rationale for the right to live according to such a dignity, and to enjoy in equity the goods of the earth. This is closely related to actions in pro of social justice, especially for those more vulnerable and/or those in a more disadvantageous situation. This is the moral basis for the activities in favor of the needy ones. It also implies a favorable attitude towards social policies. The Church can plead for the wellbeing of the aging within the larger society by supporting existent civic projects designed to benefit the aging and by promoting social policies guaranteeing the aging's financial security, adequate housing, fair retirement practices, etc.

There is another implication of the notion that all men are children of God, the consideration of men as equal parts who, according to the plan of God, are able to make a differential contribution to social life. In other words, all people are called to devote themselves, and their talents, to further the Kingdom of God. The idea is that all the people have an equal right to participate as fully as they wish, and are able to do so.

The Church, then is one institution where all ages are called with the same directness to be members. So the church may be the setting for the enriching exchange of experience, commitment, and affection among the generations.

This is true in abstract terms, but to become reality it requires the existence of a working congregation. The Catholic Church, as an association of individuals related by a common faith, used to be a corporate body much more in spiritual and symbolic terms ("mystici corporis") than in terms of a really close social relationships. This topic will be dealt with in more detail in relation with the second need.

The Need to Feel a Useful and Integrated Member of Society

In as much as one is a member of a religious community one feels integrated, at least in part, to society. Catholicism, until the last Vatican Council,[1] did not emphasize the congregational life. Since then, increasing lay participation has gradually taken root, ecclesiastical communities have been created in ever growing numbers. Elderly participation in them may, in the future, enable old people to feel as useful and integrated members of their religious community. Furthermore, their participation could increase their sense of self-worth and provide a rewarding experience that may help them to grow in pride and self-confidence. Also, their work there could help to increase in others respect for the aged. Being in a group setting can provide opportunities for friendship and sharing, and thus increase the feeling of belonging.

The existence of an increasing congregational life opens a vast range of activities where the elderly may accomplish specific tasks that would allow them to feel useful for others, to feel co-authors, each one according to his capacities, of the welfare of their brothers. In order to have the greatest impact over the wellbeing of the elderly these activities must promote the interrelationship among generations, and, at least some of them, must be oriented to help the families to take care of their aged member.

There is a last aspect that should be mentioned. Religious experience may allow the elderly believer to transcend his loneliness, in as much as he feels himself symbolically tied to the spiritual community of "mystici corporis" and related to others in all the Catholic rites (all the sacraments require the presence of others).

CONCLUSION

The prime influence of the Catholic lifestyle at present is achieved through mental constructions and exerted at the psychological level. In the future, it may also provide a network of social relations and thus increases the influence exerted at the social level.

NOTES

1. The influence of Catholicism is exerted through the process of socialization which allows the religious content to become part of the personal mode-of-being in the world of Catholics.

2. "A religion is a system of symbols, which act to establish powerful, pervasive and long lasting moods and motivation in men by formulating conceptions of a general order of existence and clothing these conceptions with such an aura of factuality that the moods and motivations seem uniquely realistic." See Clifford Geertz cited in The International Encyclopedia of the Social Sciences, MacMillan and Free Press, 1968, Vol. 13, p. 411.

3. These ideas are due to Max Weber, "Religion," in H. H. Gerth and C. Wright Mills (eds.), From Max Weber, New York, Oxford University Press, 1958 Part 111. I am aware that all Christian religions have many of these ideas in common.

On Perennial Youth and Longevity: A Taoist View on Health of the Elderly

Fumimaso Fukui

I hear the ancient people did not decline in health even when they were over one hundred years old. However the present people become decrepit at just over fifty. Why is this?

Because the present people do not pay attention to natural law, pursue pleasures and exhaust themselves before they accomplish their natural life span. On the contrary, the ancient people lived according to what they should be (chen: the Perfect), that is natural law, so they could accomplish a celestial longevity.

INTRODUCTION

This is a dialogue between the legendary Yellow Emperor, who is said to be a founder of medicine and his celestial master, Ch'i po. This tale is mentioned in the beginning of a book of medical theory of ancient China, the *Simple Questions of the Inner Book of Yellow Emperor (Huang-ti-ching su-wen)*.

This tale is representative of various legends of the Golden Age in China. It contains the common themes that since human beings grew "artful" they have never been what they used to be, and that because their life span has become short, therefore they should return to the Perfected ways of the ancient state. There are other statements: "As the ancient period was nearly a Perfected state, a disease could be cured by means of the 'sorcery' of a shaman"; or, "A holy doctor never treats those who are affected with a disease."

Permission to publish this material has been granted by the World Health Organization.

That is to say, a disease which must be treated was considered to be due to the lack of ethics.

The history of medicine in China seems to have begun with the activity of the shamans of prehistoric times. According to the archaeological literature, during the Yin dynasty (11th century B.C.), the cause of a disease was considered to be an evil consequence of demons or a divine punishment, or perhaps, a result of a change in the weather. The treatment was the task of a shaman or a witch doctor, and penitence was one of the effective measures of treatment.

The *Mo-tzu*, a book which treats the words and activities of Mo ti and his followers (the Mohists) of the fifth century B.C., mentions the God, the Director of Destiny (ssu-ming shen), who presides over the length of one's life. He is regarded as a divine messenger who decides length of life according to good and bad deeds committed. At that time such concepts were popular among not only Mohists but the general public. Also, in the ancient geography, the *Book of Mountains and Seas (Shan-hai Ching)*, a book compiled probably in the third century A.D., we can see that gods who preside over the length of one's life existed everywhere in China.

The description in the *Mo-tzu* is directed primarily to Confucians. Confucians were never eager to refer to the existence of demons, considering rather the matter of the relation between the individual and society as well as the role of morality in society. Yet they insisted that morality should depend not on a religious authority, such as Heaven or God, but on the awareness of the individual. They were of the opinion that there used to be an ideal reign by the ancient holy king in the Golden Age. Therefore, the purpose of Confucians was to restore to the original ideal system. Mohists, however, regarded as essential the elements of *real* antiquity, instead of the ideal antiquity of the Confucians. The Mohists, and other people at that time, regarded the life span of the ancients as the result of their ethics.

THE FIRST DOCTOR

The first "doctor" is considered to be Pien-ch'ueh, whose biography can be seen in the *Records of the Grand Historians of China* (Shih Chi of Ssu-ma Ch'ien, (first century B.C.). He is, however, partly a legendary person since it is described that he lived for 200 years, from the end of the sixth century B.C. So, we can suppose that his biography is in fact mixed up with stories of several doctors. Elements of a shaman remain with him, but he already used acupuncture and medicine peculiar to Chinese medicine. It is also known that moxa cautery began to be used around this time. In the biography of Pien-ch'ueh, he indicates six cases in which a disease cannot be cured. They are:

1. The case of the sick who are self-indulgent and impervious to reason;
2. The case of the sick who value money above life;
3. The case of the sick whose food and clothes are not good;
4. The case of the sick whose mental condition is unstable;
5. The case of the sick who are past cure and reject medicinal substances;
6. The case of the sick who do not trust doctors but shamans.

These are basically true in the present day, and we cannot see any cases in which the lack of ethics is the cause of a disease. The sixth case shows us that doctors at that time were nearly independent of shamanic roles. However, in the *Ho-kuan tzu*, there is the following description of Pien-ch'ueh:

Pien-ch'ueh had two brothers who were also doctors. A king asked him about their merits. He answered that his eldest was the best doctor because he could cure the person who threatened to fall ill and that his second brother was second best because he could cure a sick person instantly. As a result, the two did not become famous, while Pien-ch'ueh himself used acupuncture or medicine to cure so that he became famous, although he was the worst doctor. . . .

As we have seen, for the Chinese medicine was an act to restore the body, injured by self-indulgence, to what it should be; at the same time, medicine was a necessary evil. Medicine was also the product of man's artfulness.

TAOISTS AND NATURAL LAW

It was a school called Taoist that was most critical of their artfulness. The Taoists seem to have appeared in the third century B.C. to stand against the Confucians. As a matter of fact, it was the Taoists that began to insist on following natural law. The Confucians advocated establishing an ideal society dependent on morality. On the other hand, the Taoists advocated the reign of nonaction, as in the *Lao-tzu*, where natural law is called Tao, and in the *Chuang-tzu*, which advocates the conduct of life in a manner deduced from the workings of the Tao. The Taoists insist that men should give up every artfulness and live according to the Tao, natural law.

Natural law was considered central not only by the Taoists but also by other schools. In some cases, natural law is Heaven and in others, Law. For example, during the Han dynasty (B.C. 202-A.D. 221), it was considered that natural law appeared in the movement of a celestial sphere, in the change of weather or the four seasons, in earthquakes, and even in popular fashion, It was whatever indicated the will of Nature to human beings. Its appearance was considered to be affected by two Breaths, Yin and Yang, and was explained with Five Elements (Wood, Fire, Soil, Metal, and Water). This was the way of analysis at that time, and the whole world of nature, including the human body, was interpreted in this way. The Han was the age of reorganization of all the ancient culture, or civilization. Almost everything was rearranged with respect to natural law. To live in accord with natural law was what was expected of human beings. The famous *Book of Changes (I Ching)* was interpreted through reference to the cycles of Yin and Yang. The *I Ching* was considered to be a book by which man could know directly the change of human affairs through natural law.

THEORY OF IMMORTALITY

Before the Han period, another school was developed almost simultaneously with Taoism. A man who was free of death was called an Immortal (shen-hsien) or Perfected Man (chen-jen). It seems that ideas concerning the Immortals evolved in connection with Taoist thought. Their purpose was to complete the natural life span and to extend it to attain eternal life. It was considered that human beings would not be mortal beings if only they would follow natural law, the will of Heaven. The theory of medicine, we have seen, was influenced decisively by this theory of Immortality. Part of Taoist thought also assimilated this theory. The basic methods for becoming an Immortal seem to have already been fixed before the Han. During these years, this theory came to have so great an influence on people that even the emperor longed to become an Immortal.

This theory of Immortality deals with how one goes about living long, avoiding growing old, and avoiding dying. This current of thought adopted whatever concerned longevity. Simple ways of keeping healthy, everything concerned in following natural law, and even Buddhism, which was introduced to China from India at this time, were adopted as ways and means of longevity.

The most remarkable influence on thought about the Immortals can be seen in medicine. Pharmacology as well as medicine already had a long history, but it was not until Han times that a comprehensive compilation of pharmacy was made. After going through a series of improvements, the compilation was systematized by T'ao Hung-shenn (456-536). In his *Shen-nung Pharmacopeia (Shen-nung Pen-t'sao Ching)*, medicines are divided into three categories, as follows: the higher ones give immortality; those of the second category prolong life; those of the third category cure sickness. The book argues that the best medicines should be what makes men what they should be (Perfected), and that medicines used only for medical treatment are inferior. Here we can see again some of enduring characteristics of Chinese medicine.

T'ao Hung-shenn is supposed to be a representative figure of Taoism, the ethnic religion in China. It is a religion which teaches the pursuit of immortality and lays stress on venerating natural law, the Tao.

ETHICS

At the end of the Han, in the latter half of the second century, two sects appeared which laid emphasis on ethics. These are considered to be the origin of Taoist sects. It is noticeable that these sects insisted on a social morality similar to that of Confucians; however, it is even more noticeable that they devoted themselves to curing the sick and that they explained disease as being caused by sin. They taught that ethics was the very way for achieving long life, and their ethical code was to accord with natural law, or the Tao. They explained that sin was to violate the Tao, which was a clause of their statutes. The devotee who violated these statutes had to beg an apology from natural law.

It required a certain amount of time for the ethical Taoism of the sects to mix together with the unrestrained theories of Immortality, so the date of formation of Taoism remains to be determined. In this sense, the *Master Who Embraces Simplicity (Pao-p'u tzu)* of Ko Hung (283-343) cannot always be said to be Taoist, but it is a significant comprehensive compilation of the thought on the Immortals. In this book, Ko Hung says that the Gold Elixir (chin-tan) is the most effective method for becoming an Immortal.

Elixirs were primarily composed of the red mineral, cinnabar (mercuric sulfide). Heated and distilled, cinnabar changes into mercury of white color. Combined with oxygen, it changes into black mercuric oxide. Ko Hung explains that mercury with these properties changes into gold if mixed with various materials. This is alchemy, and it was supposed that one could gain Immortality with this gold. What is certain is that this gold is dangerous simply because it is made from mercury. In later times there are cases in which men died from eating elixir products. As a result, alchemy was called "external cinnabar" (wai-tan) in the sense that this method was made outside the body. Instead of this, "internal cinnabar" (nei-tan) came to be valued. The inner method sets value on moral training (Zen, for example) and teaches how to gain Immortality, like gold, from the inside.

LONG LIFE

In the *Pao-p'u tzu*, the Gold Elixir is considered to be the best way of achieving long life, but other ways which had been practiced since the third century B.C. are also indicated. They are divided as follows into five general categories.

A. *Avoiding cereals (pi-ku)*. One should avoid consuming any form of cereals. They contain dirty breath, and it is necessary to prevent this dirty breath from acting on the breath inside the body. Taken into consideration with the next way, a reason for this avoidance may be because cereals are annual plants.

B. *Dietary restrictions (fu-erh)*. Like pi-ku, this way is a kind of dietary cure involving living on unusual foodstuffs, such as rare kinds of fungi or nuts of pine trees which are evergreen (as opposed to the dangerous, short-lived cereals). Those who want to become Immortal should be on such an unusual diet to refresh the breath which makes up their bodies.

C. *Respiration (fu-ch'i)*. This is a kind of breathing exercise to expel the breath inside the body and to take in fresh breath. There were some practices which seem to be a kind of medication. This way later came to be associated with internal cinnabar.

D. *Kinesitherapy (tao-yin)*. This is a kind of gymnastics, like traditional Chinese shadow boxing or yoga. It is also a way of making the breath circulate in the body by assuming various poses.

E. *Sexual Hygiene (fang-chung)*. This way is apt to be misunderstood and criticized, being considered to be sexual technique in general; however, it is a way of preventing the waste of energy caused by sexual intercourse and of making the breath or essence (ching, the origin of life or energy — identified with sperm) circulate in the body. This way is mostly for men, teaching that ejaculation shortens a man's life and that men can take in the essence of women. It is also said that by taking various postures one can cure some diseases. It seems that this way had a varied content.

These ways developed further in the Taoist movements that evolved later, but the basic ones had already been established at the time of the *Pao-p'u tzu*. It is also noticeable that each way was practiced not separately, but in parallel with others.

According to the *Pao-p'u tzu*, those who aim at becoming Immortals should be ethical as well as practice those other ways. This means that they should not strictly indulge themselves in methodology. There are twenty-nine prohibitions in the *Pao-p'u tzu*, which are not always of Confucian origin but are social in nature. They may have practiced or produced the Gold Elixir in the remote mountains but social ethics were required. It was considered that the achievement of practice could not be gained without ethics and that the reason why practices sometimes failed was the lack of ethics.

Key points made in the *Pao-p'u tzu* were carried on in Taoism, which was established in the fifth century, as its basic doctrine. It was thought that physical practices and ethical ones should go together. Ko Hung was not religious, but was in fact a Confucianist and an expert on long-life practices.

A passage on ethical code in the *Pao-p'u tzu* was re-edited as the *Book of Great Superior Retribution (T'ai-shang Kan-ying p'ien)*, a book for enlightening the general public, and was published at the beginning of the Southern Sung dynasty (the middle of the 12th century). This book was very popular and headed the list of "good texts" (shan-shu). "Good texts" were popular ethical books to tell the general public to do good. Books similar to this were published until modern times. Chinese religion is represented by Confucianism, Taoism and Buddhism, but these "good texts" were preached not from any religious standpoint but from a universal standpoint of Chinese culture common to all these religions.

Another point that later came to be popular was mentioned in the *Pao-p'u-tzu*. It is the idea of a "Merit System" (Kung-kuo-ke), which means that the length of one's life is decided according to one's good and bad actions. If one commits a sin, the length of his life is shortened by some days, and if one is good, his life is lengthened. This may be the continuation of ancient Chinese views of life, but carries modern rationality. Later, this thought was developed independently to the moral self-conduct record, a "diary" of good and bad actions.

Chinese culture is said to be realistic in general and to have a peculiarity in point of pursuing human desires. However, the goal of Immortality, the highest perfection of physical desires, was accompanied by a considerable mental control, as we have seen.

Ethics and methodology were part of a single complex, adopted of necessity by the Chinese in their pursuit of well-being, which, after all, is never an easy matter to form into pat principles.

A Study of the Health of the Elderly from the Standpoint of Shinto

Takeshi Mitsuhashi

INTRODUCTION

The World Health Organization (WHO) Charter says, "Health is a perfect physical, psychological, and social condition of welfare, not just the absence of sickness or infirmity." Is Shinto, the native religion of the Japanese people, conducive to enjoying a healthy life? In other words, can we find any solution in the Shinto lifestyle and psychology to gaining such a healthy life? This paper will deal with these problems, especially concerning the elderly.

Well, we cannot discuss all the problems in one lump, for there are too many individual differences in external details and psychology, but death is a common problem that we cannot avoid when we consider the health of the elderly.

Death is always immediate for senior citizens, while it remains far off for youth. The elderly consider it a problem of great urgency. Let us look at a few examples: Hearing of the death of his friend, an elderly man's health goes suddenly downhill as he worries day after day, and at last falls ill in bed; another, who had been known to live happily with his wife, saw her die of cancer, and, as if attempting to go with her, he killed himself; another became lonely and ill after the death of his child.

Similar examples are too numerous to mention. Examining them, we can easily understand that death is an urgent problem to the

Permission to publish this material has been granted by the World Health Organization.

elderly. Whether of others or of relatives, death is a great shock, and not comparable with what young people experience. As stated before, the death of a wife can make a man feel lonely, ruin his health, and ultimately drive him to suicide. In short, therein lies the fundamental problem of death: to promote and preserve the health of the elderly, in spite of death's closeness.

SHINTO OVERCOMES THE PROBLEM OF DEATH

It goes without saying that man is mortal. Buddha also states that all creatures are mortal. Death always follows us like our shadow, but none of us know when we will die; still, death will surely come. Elderly people often say they hear death walking toward them. Some of them worry about it, and are driven to despair. Others imagine themselves in the throes of death, crying with pain. Such worries, fears, and inquietude each have untold influence on their health. Among them, the fear of death's loneliness and the inquietude that comes from not knowing the land of death are more serious. In short, the elderly seem to fear the separation or solitude of death rather than death itself. H. Kishimoto, a scholar of religion, states that death is a time for separation. Leaving family, friends, and all that is familiar, one must go to rest alone. This is a most solitary and fearful journey.

How do we live in order to be free from such fears? First of all, we should gaze at death, not fear it. Death is not at all avoidable, as Buddha has said. It is important to inscribe that in our memory. In Buddhism, especially in the Zen sect, *nen-shi*, it has been considered one of the important exercises, to have a true realization of death. The Samurai class, who daily faced death, also knew how to live positively through gazing steadily at death. Such a view of life and death has been common to various religions and beliefs of Asia. Japanese Shinto is not an exception.

It is generally said that Shinto is a religion based on ceremonial rites and festivals (*matsuri*), most of which center on the rice crop. Among them, the Toshi-gohi no matsuri (*Kinensai*) — the Grain-petitioning Festival — held in February, and the Nihi-name no matsuri (*Shinjosai*) — the New Grain Banquet Festival — in November are the most important. The Toshi-gohi no matsuri petitions for the abundance of grain, and the Nihi-name no matsuri gives thanks for the harvest. This pair of festivals is expected to renew the power of all creatures, for rice is regarded as a symbol of life. For the Japanese people, one year has always been synonymous with the life cycle of rice: it is sowed in spring, grows in summer, is harvested in autumn, and dies in winter.

Here I need to explain that the death of rice does not mean ending, but renewal. It is similar to a famous parable in the Bible: unless a grain of wheat falls into the earth and dies, it remains alone; but if it dies, it bears much fruit.

There are various festivals in Japan which are repeated annually for renewal of life. It is essential in Shinto to hold these festivals and cyclical ceremonies faithfully every year to realize the renewal and, further, the eternity of life through them.

Summing up, life and death are two sides of the same thing. Realizing that, people can come to perceive eternity as meaning neither life nor death, and then live a positive life. At this time, the problem of death is solved, and the health of the elderly can be preserved and promoted, I suppose.

However civilized or prosperous nations are, or however well equipped medical facilities are, people are not exempt from the fear of death. In respect to this fear, the Shinto lifestyle and psychology seem to be especially useful.

SHINTO AND SOLITUDE

Next, we will consider the problem of solitude. It cannot be denied that the older people are, the more they feel isolated. As stated above, such a feeling is bad for one's health for various reasons. Here, we will consider how Shinto is useful in overcoming this isolation.

Shinto is obviously polytheistic. The countryside in Japan is dotted with many *jinja* (Shinto shrines) where various *kami* (gods) are enshrined. Each *kami* (god) has his own territory, where the community of believers is organized by blood ties or territorial ones. The *kami* or the *jinja* fills the role of tutelary deity, protecting his own community from evil spirits and keeping the community happy. But he never seeks to broaden nor to narrow his territory, nor does he invade others. His activity is limited, which is, I think, a worthwhile feature of Shinto. In this point, it is different from Christianity, which is propagated to all the world.

This is true of Amaterasu Omikami, the supreme goddess. By the *Nihonshoki*, the oldest myth history, published in 720, she was born to be a lord. It also says in the *Kogoshui* written in 807, that her holiness is matchless. From the beginning, she was regarded as the holiest, which came to be interpreted exaggeratedly through the middle and modern ages. In books of those times, she was considered the parent or the supreme tutelary of Japan. The Ise Jingu (Grand Shrine of Ise), dedicated to her, was worshiped by all the Japanese people, and everyone was eager to make a pilgrimage there at least once in his lifetime.

Therefore, her territory and activity are supposed to cover Japan proper. It is worthy of our notice that there are different gods, with their territories, within her domain. In other words, she allows them to live in every part of her kingdom. They are not only kami (Shinto gods) but also Buddhist and Christian. We should take into consideration that her activity, pervading over all the land, never invades the territories of other religions. In a word, it is rare that we find the idea of conquest in Shinto as we do in other universal religions. It prefers coexistence and co-prosperity to fighting. In such a coexistent society, people respect each other, so that they never feel lonely. What is more, they coexist with surrounding nature instead of despoiling it.

Japanese people have conceived since ancient times that every natural element (seas, mountains, rivers, grass, trees, rocks, and so on) has its own holy spirit, and it is thus a god in itself. We can read in the *Nihonshoki* and the *Norito*, ritual prayers written in archaic times, that all trees and grass are able to speak. This concept still prevails. For example, if a pine tree is obstructed by a fence, people usually bore a hole in the fence to permit growth of the tree; people still tell a legend of a stone weeping in the night; there are pairs of rocks or pine trees called husband and wife all over Japan. Similar examples are numberless. The first example illustrates coexistence. In the other two we find the idea that rocks or trees have the same spirits as men, which is related to the idea that a god exists in every natural object or phenomenon. Such aspects of a Shinto lifestyle as recognizing all creatures and coexisting with them, seem to relieve the loneliness of the elderly.

Coexistence might be possible in a polytheistic society, but a monotheistic religion never recognizes other gods as objects of faith, only its own, so that it is not easy to coexist even ideally.

It is often said that Japanese people are either irreligious or half-hearted toward religion, but that is a one-sided view. As stated before, we believe in the god's existence in every natural object or phenomenon and worship it. It appears to me that Japanese people are actually rather pious. For instance, not a few elderly people worship kami (gods) and their ancestors enshrined on the family altars every day. Putting photos of their ancestors there, they often speak to them as if the ancestors were present, for they believe the ancestors visit this world.

Japanese people are not confronted by their kami, their ancestors, or their parents, but respect and coexist with them through a Shinto lifestyle. Realizing this coexistence, old people can come to feel ease and enjoy completely good health.

On the other hand, it is true that the fear of divine punishment is bad for health. This is a serious problem for the elderly, related to the land of death. In order to solve this problem of fear, it is of foremost importance to live with sincerity. This important ideal of Shinto means to have a clear, right, and honest mind; to live impartially, neither feeling guilty nor ashamed of oneself in the presence of the god.

In conclusion, I consider it good for the health of the elderly to lead such an impartial life; the Shinto lifestyle and psychology of coexistence and simple sincerity are beneficial for health.

Religious Factors in Aging, Adjustment, and Health: A Theoretical Overview

Jeffrey S. Levin

INTRODUCTION

For nearly thirty years, gerontologists have explored the relationship over the life cycle between religious participation and measures of health and well-being, such as subjective health and person adjustment. However, findings are often contradictory, and the evidence linking religious behavior to health and well-being is largely inconclusive.[1] A major explanation for this may lie in the general lack of attention to theoretical issues in many of these studies. While the empirical literature on religion and health in social gerontology is less atheoretical than its counterpart in social epidemiology,[2] sociologists of religion have apparently neglected this field of inquiry.[3] The work of those scholars who have written in this area appears to be founded in several somewhat overlapping theoretical orientations. Implicit in each of these perspectives are expectations regarding the ways in which aging affects both the intensity of reli-

Jeffrey S. Levin is with the Institute of Gerontology, University of Michigan, Ann Arbor, MI 48109.

The author wishes to acknowledge Dr. Kyriakos S. Markides for his comments on an earlier version of this manuscript, which was presented to the Gerontological Health Section at the Annual Meeting of the American Public Health Association, Washington, DC, November, 1985.

gious involvement and the salience of religion to health and well-being.

This paper will identify six theoretical viewpoints which have guided gerontological research on religion and health. Each of these offers different predictions regarding the (changing) nature of the relationship between religion and health as people grow old. These perspectives include activity theory, a "deterioration" perspective, the social decrement or isolation model, disengagement theory, an "eschatological" perspective, and the multidimensional disengagement perspective of Mindel and Vaughan.[4]

Next, empirical findings addressing religion, health, and aging will be critically reviewed. Nearly twenty such studies have appeared in recent years, and their findings will be considered in light of the expectations of the competing perspectives. Finally, some conclusions will be drawn as to which set of predictions appears to most closely account for the data.

ALTERNATIVE THEORETICAL ORIENTATIONS

In attempting to understand how religion and health are associated as people grow old, it is apparent that there are two rather distinct dimensions to this problem. On the one hand, there is the matter of religion's salience to health—that is, the strength of a religion and health relationship. As people age, does this association grow stronger? Does it weaken? Does it remain unchanged? Furthermore, does religion relinquish its "therapeutic significance"[5] at some point in the life cycle? In other words, does religious involvement lose its epidemiologically significant protective value[6] and begin to take on the characteristics of a risk factor?

On the other hand, there is the matter of religious involvement itself. Independent of its (changing) salience to health, evidence suggests that patterns of religious activity change to some extent as people age. However, there are conflicting findings in this area[7] due to the infrequent differentiation of organized religious activity (i.e., activity outside the home, such as religious attendance) from "non-organizational" types of religious involvement, such as prayer and religious feelings, as well as the other sorts of religious behavior engaged in by shut-ins (e.g., watching the PTL Club in lieu of attending services). Nevertheless, the issue remains that any examination of religion and health, in an aging context, must address religious involvement per se as independent of its salience to health. In other words, when considering the effects on health of either organizational or nonorganizational religious involvement, one must also determine whether such activity increases or decreases with increasing age.

The literature suggests that there are at least six potential ways in which a religion and health relationship may behave as people grow older. These competing perspectives will now be briefly outlined. It should be stressed that these are not discrete theoretical perspectives. Rather, they are alternative sets of expectations governing religious involvement and its relationship to health and well-being as people age.

One perspective takes a decidedly "eschatological" view. Namely, this orientation suggests that, as people grow old, they face numerous crises (e.g., retirement, loss of wealth, declining health, loss of power, bereavement, etc.) — crises which challenge the very assumptions which may have guided one's life. Some people are then led to take an inventory of their life as they begin to prepare for their inevitable demise. This preparation may involve an increase in religious involvement.[8] Furthermore, religion may take on a much more dominant role in one's life. Religious considerations will become increasingly more salient as one makes adjustments in his or her style of life, and religion may become an increasingly powerful determinant of one's health and well-being. This eschatological perspective is characteristic of work in theology and religion, especially that which looks favorably to the "cure of souls" as a pastoral role of increasing importance as people steer their way through life.[9] In sum, this perspective predicts increased religious involvement, both organizational and nonorganizational, and expects this involvement to be increasingly salient to health and well-being.

Another possible radix of expectations governing the relationship between religion and health as people age is a "deterioration" perspective. This is similar in many respects to the previous orientation, yet diverges slightly. This perspective suggests that, as people grow old, they deteriorate physically and mentally, leading them to seek out religion as a source of comfort or even healing. However, disability and concomitant activity limitation should limit their ability to participate in organized religious activities. Therefore, nonorganizational religious behavior and heightened religiosity should take its place. For these reasons, poorer health should be associated with both decreased religious attendance and increased religiosity, and these associations should grow stronger with age, as people grow less healthy and more devout and attend church less. While this perspective is often not explicitly stated, it is implicit in studies offering conclusions such as, "Apparently, if frail elderly persons overcome their health limitations sufficiently to attend religious services, they experience considerable happiness, excitement, and satisfaction in their lives. But regular attendance makes little difference to the well-being of healthy older people."[10]

In sum, this perspective predicts decreased organizational religious involvement and increased nonorganizational involvement. In addition, the association between health and organizational religion should grow increasingly stronger in a positive direction as religious attendance becomes increasingly a proxy for health status. Furthermore, the association between health and nonorganizational religion should also grow increasingly stronger, but in a negative direction.

A third perspective on religion, health, and aging is provided by activity theory, which suggests that, as folks age, they slough old activities, trading them for new ones such as renewed religious attendance. This increased vigor of religious activity can occur late in life, or may commence at an earlier age with the arrival of marriage and children. In either event, religious attendance then begins a steady rise which persists until the very oldest ages, when disability leads to decline. This view is quite reminiscent of what has been labelled the "traditional model" of the relationship between religious attendance and aging, in contradistinction to other models which predict a general decline in religious attendance with age.[11] However, an activity perspective does not presume that religion, per se, represents any more or less salient determinant of health and well-being as people age. In other words, while religious attendance might increase, the association between religion and health should not necessarily change in intensity. In sum, this perspective predicts that, up until the very oldest ages, organizational religious involvement will increase, yet be neither more nor less salient to health and well-being.

Another perspective on this issue is provided by disengagement theory. This influential theoretical orientation[12] suggests that, as people get older, they voluntarily disengage from society and social institutions, including organized religion. These institutions play less significant roles in their lives, and one would expect, then, that religion would become less salient a factor to one's health and well-being. This perspective, though, has been criticized on the grounds that it ignores the subjective or affective (attitudinal) dimension of social relationships.[13] In other words, individuals may disengage formally, yet, informally remain highly involved in the social relationship or institutions from which they appear, on the surface, to have disengaged. These comments suggest at least two additional perspectives on the relationship between religion, health, and aging, both spin-offs of disengagement theory.

One such perspective is the social decrement or isolation model, which, like disengagement theory, anticipates a decline in religious attendance as people get older. However, unlike disengagement, this perspective raises the issue of acquiescence to disengagement; meaning, this withdrawal from social relationships and social institutions may not actually be desired. In other words, some older people become socially isolated against their will, and due to any number of reasons — living alone, lack of transportation, institutionalization, few surviving friends in church, the increasing secularization of religious services, etc. — they may be unable to participate actively in organized religious activity. However, this notion that older people may disengage yet not "go quietly" suggests that, in this case, religion may not necessarily decline in its salience to health or to life satisfaction in general. In fact, because religion may still be important, yet formally practiced to a lesser extent, disengagement from religious attendance may transpire only to the detriment of one's general well-being.

For example, much of the early work of Moberg linked church

membership and attendance in older people to better personal adjustment.[14] What, then, would be the fate of such folks if they could not attend church? Moberg[15] suggests that when organized religious activity declines it is replaced by heightened religious feelings. However, one study noted that isolated older people do not necessarily rely more upon religion than other older people.[16] Regardless, this social decrement perspective is conceptually differentiable from disengagement theory, and its expectations merit separate presentation. In sum, this perspective predicts decreased organizational religious involvement, which is an increasingly salient determinant of poor health. However, unlike the "deterioration" perspective, this strengthened association is not merely the result of the increasing identity of religious attendance as a proxy for health. Rather, declines in religious attendance are themselves considered detrimental to health.

A sixth and final theoretical orientation, and like the decrement model, a variation of disengagement theory, is the multidimensional disengagement perspective suggested by Mindel and Vaughan.[4] This orientation is founded in the observation that aging is accompanied by a decrease in organizational religious involvement, yet an increase in nonorganizational involvement (e.g., prayer, listening to religious music, reading the Bible, etc.). Therefore, while consistent with disengagement theory and contrary to the social decrement perspective, religious attendance should grow less salient a factor in health, this multidimensional orientation suggests an increase in the strength of the association between health and some types of nonorganizational religious involvement due to the increased disability of older people. In sum, this perspective predicts increased nonorganizational religious involvement, which is of increasing salience to health.

Nearly twenty published studies in social gerontology have given empirical attention to the relationship of religious factors to health and well-being. Findings bearing on the (changing) relationship between religion, adjustment, and health across the life cycle will now be reviewed in order to determine which of the six competing perspectives best predicts how religion and health covary as people grow old.

REVIEW OF EMPIRICAL FINDINGS

Religious Involvement

Evidence from various settings demonstrates that, contrary to the deterioration, social decrement, and disengagement perspectives, religious involvement does not generally decline as people age except with respect to religious attendance and only among those individuals with a serious disability. Markides and his associates[1] have noted that despite contradictory, ambiguous, and inconclusive results characterizing research in religion and aging, the stability of religious involvement including religious attendance in most older people is one finding which "has been established with some certainty" (p. 67).

In a longitudinal study of older Anglos and Mexican Americans, Markides[17] determined that religious attendance is relatively stable as older people age. Ortega et al.,[18] in a study in Alabama, found the frequency of church-related visits to be fairly consistent during adulthood and old age. In a recent study of older Mennonites, Ainlay and Smith[19] found only a partial disengagement of organizational religious activity, and this was offset by increases in nonorganizational, private religious activities. The authors thus conclude that total religious disengagement does not occur as people grow old, and furthermore, that religion retains its salience in old age. Finally, Heisel and Faulkner,[20] in a study of middle-aged and older Blacks, found that church membership and attendance increase slightly with age while religiosity remains constant. However, these findings are based upon cross-sectional data, suggesting that even the minor increase in religious attendance may reflect a cohort effect.

In sum, it appears that religious attendance is fairly stable throughout life, and may decline only in the very old whose physical activity has been limited by disability. In addition, notwithstanding these declines in organizational religious involvement, personal religious activity remains stable and may even increase somewhat with age.

Religion, Adjustment, and Health

Findings linking religious activity to health and well-being are mixed. However, negative findings (i.e., nonsignificant associations) reported by some studies may be unreliable for a number of reasons. A 30-year-old study[21] reported no significant differences between religious adjustment and both health and total adjustment. However, institutionalized and noninstitutionalized subjects were combined, nearly all of the subjects were females, what was meant by "religious adjustment" is uncertain, and the failure to detect a significant difference may have been a function of insufficient statistical power (there were only 32 noninstitutionalized subjects). In a study completed a quarter century ago,[22] religious activity and a physician-rated functional health index were not significantly associated. However, the religious activity variable did not differentiate between organizational and nonorganizational activity, perhaps obscuring a significant relationship. A more recent study using National Opinion Research Center (NORC) data[23] found nonsignificant zero-order associations between life satisfaction and church attendance. However, life satisfaction was measured by only a single item in contrast to the more conventional use of scales.

Reports of statistically significant associations between religion and health and well-being are of two types. First, three studies have linked religious attendance to general measures of personal adjustment or well-being. In a longitudinal study of older people, Keith[24] found that subjects who had experienced continuity in religious attendance were more likely to have positive attitudes toward life than were those who had experienced a decremental change in attendance. Furthermore, these "positivists" and "activists" were also likelier to have maintained their health. In the Duke Longitudinal Study of Aging, Blazer and Palmore[25] found that religious activities, including church attendance, correlated significantly with personal adjustment, while "religious attitudes" did not. Using NORC data, Steinitz[10] found that religious attendance, but not self-rated religiosity, was consistently associated with well-being. Similar findings were obtained longitudinally by Markides.[17] In sum, among older people organizational religious involvement is positively related to well-being, and this relationship does not appear to decline with age.

Second, there is some evidence that nonorganizational religious involvement may, in fact, be inversely related to well-being in the aged, although findings are mixed. A positive association is suggested by two studies,[26] and by another study[27] in which a negative association with "psychic well-being" reversed after controls were added, though it failed to attain significance. However, one recent study revealed a strong negative association between religiosity and well-being. In their research on older adults, Mindel and Vaughan[4] found that nonorganizational religious involvement was greater among those whose health impairment was greatest. In sum, these findings demonstrate that the relationship between nonorganizational religious involvement and health and well-being in older people may be in a negative direction. However, results are inconclusive, and an inverse association certainly should not be taken as evidence that subjective religiosity leads to poorer health. Rather, declines in health might engender heightened private expressions of religiosity.

A third group of positive findings deals specifically with measures of life satisfaction. In a study of men and women aged 45 and over, Edwards and Klemmack[28] found that the intensity of church-related involvement was significantly related to life satisfaction. Furthermore, these results persisted after controlling for every other variable in their dataset, including perceived health. A recently published report[29] of a bi-racial study of adults aged 60 and over found that church attendance strongly predicts life satisfaction. As in the previous study, the analysis controlled for health, in this case a measure of functional health. In sum, organizational religious involvement is strongly related to life satisfaction in older adults.

Fourth, a couple of recent studies have linked religious attendance directly to health. Markides et al.[1] found a strong, significant, positive association between religious attendance and both subjective health and a health index. The authors note that, as people grow older, religious attendance and subjective religiosity become increasingly differentiated. They suggest that organizational religious involvement may increasingly become a proxy for functional health or the ability to perform the activities of daily living. More recently,

Levin and Markides[30] found that the relationship between religious attendance and subjective health is significant only among older people. In sum, among older people, religious attendance is significantly related to health.

SUMMARY

In summarizing all of the above findings, the nature of the relationship between religion, adjustment, and health as people age begins to emerge:

1. Religious attendance is fairly stable over the life cycle, and then may decline slightly among the very old or disabled.
2. Nonorganizational religious involvement and subjective religiosity remain stable as people age, but may increase slightly to offset those eventual declines in organizational religious involvement.
3. Nonorganizational religious involvement may be inversely related to health and well-being in older people, although results are mixed.
4. Among older people, religious attendance is positively related to general measures of personal adjustment and this association does not appear to decline with age.
5. Among older people, religious attendance is positively related to both subjective health and life satisfaction, the latter measured by either single items or scales.

CONCLUSIONS

It is apparent that these findings fit none of the six competing perspectives exactly. However, it is also apparent that Mindel and Vaughan's multidimensional disengagement perspective comes the closest. This theory suggests that, as people grow old, they disengage from organized religious activities such as attending religious services, and make up for this loss by increasing their nonorganizational religious involvement. While such expectations may be a bit overstated, the data do suggest that these predictions may work quite well among the very old, where religious attendance declines somewhat and where self-rated religiosity may increase slightly.

This multidimensional disengagement perspective also anticipates that nonorganizational religious involvement might become more strongly related to health in older people. This is, in fact, just the position the data support, although the relationship is possibly an inverse one (i.e., higher nonorganizational religious involvement may be associated with poorer health). However, the issue of causality remains unresolved. As mentioned earlier, these findings should not necessarily be taken as evidence of an increased, detrimental salience of religiosity to health in old age. Rather, as Mindel and Vaughan[4] themselves note, "Apparently being ill does not draw one away from religion but perhaps draws one to it in a more subjective, personal way" (p. 107). In other words, the increased significant association with age may be due to less healthy people becoming more religious.

Future social gerontological research into religion and health should attempt to clarify these findings. In particular, several tasks presents themselves to investigators. These include the need for longitudinal studies, the inclusion of more than one outcome variable, the use of multidimensional measures of religious involvement, and attention to theoretical issues.

First, longitudinal studies are needed to clarify the causal relationship between nonorganizational religious involvement and health and well-being. Results from cross-sectional studies may leave the impression that such religious involvement has adverse effects upon health. In reality, the possibility that sicker people become more subjectively religious may explain such findings, but a longitudinal design would be needed to confirm this. In addition, there is some recent evidence of a significant period effect.[31]

Second, the outcome variables considered here—health status, subjective health, life satisfaction, general measures of personal adjustment—are a rather heterogeneous lot. Although the relationships between these constructs and religious involvement are quite similar, it would be desirable to include measures of each within a single study. Significant paths between religion and health status could then be determined after controlling for subjective health, life satisfaction, and adjustment. A path-analytic approach would permit the calculation of direct and indirect effects.

Third, neither organizational nor nonorganizational religious involvement is a unidimensional construct. There are innumerable measures of each, and investigators should not limit themselves to just religious attendance and subjective religiosity. One might also consider Sunday School attendance, holding a church office, attendance at Wednesday night prayer meetings, Sunday School teaching, frequency of Bible study, watching religious television, private prayer, even missionary work. Then again, one might move beyond religious involvement altogether and broach issues of religious ideology and belief. Of course, a substantial barrier to the inclusion of such variables is that much of the empirical social gerontological work on religion and health has been spun-off from larger studies of health and well-being, where the inclusion of more than a few token religion variables is highly unusual.

Finally, some clarification is needed of the theoretical bases for these findings. The multidimensional disengagement perspective comes the closest to anticipating the way in which religion and health are interrelated as people age. However, it is possible that other variables left unconsidered here might explain away these results. For example, studies of religious attendance and health must avoid basing conclusions solely upon zero-order analyses. According to Levin and Markides,[32] this is an especially serious issue in studies of older people, where religious attendance may represent a proxy for functional health, or disability. A significant, uncontrolled association between religious attendance and health may mean only that older people who are healthy enough to do so. Such tautological conclusions can probably be avoided through higher-order analyses.

Alternatively, the associations between religious involvement and health and well-being might be different within different strata of society. Or, furthermore, findings might vary depending upon the religious affiliation of the subjects. Nearly all of the subjects in the studies reviewed here were either Protestants or Catholics. Until these issues are addressed, the true relationships between religion, aging, adjustment, and health will remain somewhat obscured.

NOTES

1. K.S. Markides and H.W. Martin with E. Gomez, Older Mexican Americans: A Study in an Urban Barrio (Austin: University of Texas Press, 1983).

2. See J. S. Levin and P. L. Schiller, "Is There a Religious Factor in Health?" Journal of Religion and Health, 26 (1987), pp 9-36.

3. E. F. Heenan, "Sociology of Religion and the Aged: The Empirical Lacunae," Journal for the Scientific Study of Religion, 2 (1972), 171-176.

4. C. H. Mindel and C. E. Vaughan, "A Multidimensional Approach to Religiosity and Disengagement," Journal of Gerontology, 33 (1978), 103-108.

5. H. Y. Vanderpool, "Is Religion Therapeutically Significant?" Journal of Religion and Health, 16 (1977), 255-259.

6. K. Vaux, "Religion and Health," Preventive Medicine, 5 (1976), 522-536.

7. K. S. Markides and T. Cole, "Change and Continuity in Mexican American Religious Behavior: A Three-Generation Study," Social Science Quarterly, 65 (1984), 618-625.

8. R. Stark, "Age and Faith: A Changing Outlook or an Old Process?" Sociological Analysis, 29 (1968), 1-10.

9. W.A. Clebsch, "American Religion and the Cure of Souls," 249-265 in Religion in America, W. G. McLoughlin and R. N. Bellah, eds. (Boston: Beacon Press, 1968).

10. L. Y. Steinitz, "Religiosity, Well-Being, and Weltanschauung among the Elderly," Journal for the Scientific Study of Religion, 19 (1980), 62.

11. C. R. Wingrove and J. P. Alston, "Age, Aging, and Church Attendance," The Gerontologist, pt. 1 (1971), 356-358.

12. E. Cumming and W. Henry, Growing Old: The Process of Disengagement (New York: Basic Books, 1961).

13. A. Hochschild, "Disengagement Theory: A Critique and Proposal," American Sociological Review, 40 (1975), 533-569.

14. David O. Moberg made several excellent contributions in this area in the 1950s. These include: "The Christian Religion and Personal Adjustment in Old Age," American Sociological Review, 18 (1953), 87-90; "Church Membership and Personal Adjustment in Old Age," Journal of Gerontology, 8 (1953) 1, 207-211; "Leadership in the Church and Personal Adjustment in Old Age," Sociology and Social Research, 37 (1953), 184-185; "Religious Activities and Old Age," Religious Education, 48 (1953), 184-185; "Religious Activities and Personal Adjustment in Old Age," Journal of Social Psychology, 43 (1956), 261-267; and "Christian Beliefs and Personal Adjustment to Old Age," American Scientific Affiliation Journal, 10 (1958), 8-12.

15. D. O. Moberg, "Religiosity in Old Age," The Gerontologist, 5, 2 (1965), 78-87, 111.

16. C. T. O'Reilly, "Religious Practice and Personal Adjustment of Older People," Sociology and Social Research, 42 (1957), 119-121.

17. K. S. Markides, "Aging, Religiosity, and Adjustment: A Longitudinal Analysis," Journal of Gerontology, 38 (1983), 621-625.

18. S. T. Ortega, R. D. Crutchfield, and W. A. Rushing, "Race Differences in Elderly Personal Well-Being: Friendship, Family, and Church," Research on Aging, 5 (1983), 101-118.

19. S. C. Ainlay and D. R. Smith, "Aging and Religious Participation," Journal of Gerontology, 39 (1984), 357-363.

20. M. A. Heisel and A. O. Faulkner, "Religiosity in an Older Black Population," The Gerontologist, 22 (1982), 354-358.

21. J. R. Lepkowski, "The Attitudes and Adjustments of Institutionalized and Non-Institutionalized Catholic Aged," Journal of Gerontology, 11 (1956), 185-191.

22. F. C. Jeffers and C. R. Nichols, "The Relationship of Activities and Attitudes to Physical Well-Being in Older People," Journal of Gerontology, 16 (1961), 67-70.

23. E. Spreitzer and E. E. Snyder, "Correlates of Life Satisfaction among the Aged," Journal of Gerontology, 29 (1974), 454-458.

24. P. M. Keith, "Life Changes and Perceptions of Life and Death among Older Men and Women," Journal of Gerontology, 34 (1979), 870-878.

25. D. Blazer and E. Palmore, "Religion and Aging in a Longitudinal Panel," The Gerontologist, 16, 12, pt. 1 (1976), 82-85.

26. L. J. Beckman and B. B. Houser, "The Consequences of Childlessness on the Social-Psychological Well-Being of Older Women," Journal of Gerontology, 37 (1982), 243-250; and, R. W. Bortner and D. F. Hultsch, "A Multivariate Analysis of Correlates of Life Satisfaction in Adulthood," Journal of Gerontology, 25 (1970), 41-47.

27. V. Tellis-Nayak, "The Transcendent Standard: The Religious Ethos of the Rural Elderly," The Gerontologist, 22 (1982), 359-363.

28. J. N. Edwards and D. L. Klemmack, "Correlates of Life Satisfaction: A Re-Examination," Journal of Gerontology, 28 (1973), 497-502.

29. W. M. Usui, T. J. Keil, and K. R. Durig, "Socioeconomic Comparisons and Life Satisfaction of Elderly Adults," Journal of Gerontology, 40 (1985), 110-114.

30. J. S. Levin and K. S. Markides, "Religion and Health in Mexican Americans," Journal of Religion and Health, 24 (1985), 60-69.

31. R. A. Witter, W. A. Stock, M. A. Okun, and M. J. Haring, "Religion and Subjective Well-Being in Adulthood: A Quantitative Synthesis," Review of Religious Research, 26 (1985), 332-342.

32. J. S. Levine and K. S. Markides, "Religious Attendance and Subjective Health," Journal for the Scientific Study of Religion, 25 (1986), 31-40.